LOVE LETTER TO JOHNNY FROM LANA...

"Sweetheart, please keep well, because I need you so—and so you will always be strong and able to caress me, hold me, tenderly at first, and crush me into your very own being....

My Beloved Love, just this morning your precious exciting letter arrived. . . . Every line warms me and makes me ache and miss you each tiny moment—and it's true— it's beautiful, yet terrible. But, just so is deep love. . . . Hold me, dear lover. . . ."

Soon after this, Johnny Stompanato was dead. Killed by Lana's own daughter, Cheryl Crane.

HOLLYWOOD TRAGEDY

WILLIAM H. A. CARR

A FAWCETT CREST BOOK

Fawcett Publications, Inc., Greenwich, Connecticut

HOLLYWOOD TRAGEDY

A Fawcett Crest Book published by arrangement with the Author.

Copyright © 1962, 1976 by William H. A. Carr

ISBN 0-449-22889-4

Printed in the United States of America

First Printing: July 1976

1 2 3 4 5 6 7 8 9 10

CONTENTS

1 The Star-Crossed

This is, unabashedly, a book of scandals, from Olive Thomas and Fatty Arbuckle to Bruce Lee and Judy Garland, a book about the legions of star-crossed men and women who sometimes found riches and fame in Hollywood, but often discovered, too, shame and terror and fears of failure more dreadful than the worst reality.

Sex is in this book. Crime fills many of its pages. All of the subject matter is sensational.

The popular hypocrisy of these supposedly uninhibited times still asserts that none of these things should be confessed. Books can be published about sex, crime, and other sensational matters, but they should always display a pious façade, like a Hollywood movie that carefully punishes its leading character in the last reel after salivating over the appetizing and rewarding pleasures of his sins in the previous reels.

One result of this attitude is a historical view of Hollywood that bears little semblance of reality. Read almost any of the standard histories of the motion picture industry and you'll get the impression that everyone in it—from producers to stage-hands—was a serious, sober, stable, dedicated disciple of the film as an art form. This is as much a fantasy as untrue to life, but not nearly as entertaining, as a Busby Berkeley musical of the 1930s. Hollywood was, and remains, to a considerable (but lesser) extent, a city of dreams.

This was Cinderella City, a place of legends, where a buxom girl in a tight sweater might be "discovered" by a talent scout and be turned into a movie queen overnight; where a kid from the slums might suddenly find himself earning millions of dollars; where people were debonair and beautiful and bright and glamorous—a world where an illegitimate girl with the drab name of Norma Jean, a product of wretched foster homes which had crushed and debauched her, might be magically transformed into the Goddess of Beauty, Marilyn Monroe. It was, in the felicitous phrase of sociologist Hortense Powdermaker, "the dream factory," but the factory itself became a part of the dreams it produced, so that it was well nigh impossible to distinguish between cause and effect, between the product and the producer, between the dream and the dreamer.

The dream created the Clara Bows, the Frances Farmers, the Marilyn Monroes, the Judy Garlands; they in turn became part of the dream and helped elucidate and elaborate the dream to others. And in time the dream consumed them. Olive Thomas, the Ziegfeld Girl described by a foremost artist as "the most beautiful girl in the world," unhappily married to Mary Pickford's brother Jack, enjoyed a second honeymoon with him, toured the Parisian dives, and swallowed poison after they returned to their hotel. It was called an accident. Clara Bow's mind broke when her career began to hit the skids. Carole Landis, weary of her own leg art, burdened with debt, worried about her fading career. Heartbroken because Rex Harrison wouldn't marry her, she committed suicide with sleeping pills. Barbara La Marr died of an overdose of drugs.

Women were not the only persons consumed by the dream; men were shattered and devoured by it, too. Big, handsome Wallace Reid died in a hospital where he was trying to kick his narcotics addiction. Rudolph Valentino, the "Great Lover," torn by anguish over his sexual impotence, developed massive ulcers that eventually made an operation necessary; peritonitis resulted, and the fantasy man of romance died, a victim, at least in part, of his own myths. Ramon Novarro, who

Alla Nazimova and Rudolph Valentino in *Camille*. She and his wife, Natacha Rambova, tried to make a fop of him so he turned for solace to Pola Negri.

The Museum of Modern Art/ Film Stills Archive

Rudolph Valentino and Mae Murray. She got so mad at Erich Von Stroheim that she stormed off the set with no clothes on. Dressed or undressed, Valentino made hearts throb. *The Museum of Modern Art/Film Stills Archive*

was, as Ezra Goodman said, "one of the legendary Lotharios of early-day Hollywood," remained a handsome actor, still in demand, until 1968, when he was murdered by two men who preyed on homosexuals.

For them, as for many others, the dream of glitter town had turned into a tawdry nightmare. But for millions upon millions of people not only in the United States and Canada, but in every other country in the world, the nightmares of everyday life were assuaged by the beguiling dreams of Hollywood. Moviegoers vicariously sinned, loved, fought, killed, reigned, sacrificed—all on an epic scale denied them in their ordinary, humdrum lives. The weary shopgirl could watch Clara Bow display "It" and have all the men throwing themselves at her feet, and somehow the shopgirl's life was a little brighter and more endurable. And the service station grease monkey could watch Valentino sweep the beautiful leading lady up onto the silver saddle, gallop off to his hidden oasis for a spot of gallant, genteel rape, and imagine that it was he, and not Valentino, up there on the flickering screen, behaving so romantically. The fact that Clara Bow, off-screen, posed for raunchy photographs, was famous for her real-life love affairs, and lived with insouciant flamboyance did nothing to diminish the impact of the audience's fantasies, of course. Nor did the 30,000 hysterical women who rioted outside the Frank E. Campbell Funeral Chapel in Manhattan at the time of Valentino's last rites. Clara Bow was the shopgirl, living with the reckless defiance of convention that the shopgirl longed to display. And those thousands of screaming women at Campbell's were really breaking their hearts over the grease monkey.

Hollywood won such an intimate place for itself in the hearts of moviegoers that everything its stars did, off screen as well as on, became a matter of the greatest interest. Even today, when we look back to the golden days of Hollywood, most of us remember, not merely the great movies—although they remain an important part of our culture—but also the scandals. Remember the big fuss over *Confidential* magazine? The Errol Flynn rape trial? The time that Lana Turner's daughter stabbed hoodlum Johnny Stompanato to death in her mother's bedroom? Charlie Chaplin's paternity and Mann Act trials? Ingrid Bergman's startling love affair with Roberto Rossellini? The mysterious death of Thelma Todd? The rumors when Jean Harlow's husband was found shot to death under very strange circumstances? The murder of William Desmond Taylor, which gave unwanted publicity to Mary Miles Minter and Mabel Normand? The Fatty Arbuckle trials after a bit actress died during an orgy? The questions raised when Marilyn Monroe apparently committed suicide? The horror of the savage murders of Sharon Tate and her friends? The strange cult that arose after the untimely death of James Dean?

Those are the highlights that come to mind when Hollywood's past is the subject of conversation. Even in the formal histories some scant mention of a few of them can be found. One of the best of these works, for example, says, "Late in 1922 . . . within the space of a few short months, there came in quick succession the sordid Fatty Arbuckle rape case, the mysterious and still unsolved murder of director William Desmond Taylor (implicating both Mary Miles Minter and Mabel Normand, two top box-office stars of the time), and the shocking revelation of handsome Wallace Reid's addiction to drugs. Public indignation swelled to alarming proportions. Although their outrage was directed against individuals (Arbuckle and Miss Minter never appeared in films again; Mabel Normand's career was permanently damaged), the protests rapidly assumed the form of a threatened national censorship of all movies." This was obviously a critical time for motion pictures. The furor reached all the way to the White House. (When Robert Redford brought out a film about the Watergate scandal a half century later Hollywood was able to turn the tables on Washington.) For two years or more the movie scandals and the threat of censorship were the biggest news of all, even on Page One of the august *New York Times,* which was not quite as stuffy in those days as it is today.

Despite this enormous public uproar, the motion picture history just cited contains not another word about these matters.

Presumably a child under ten would not remember anything about the Arbuckle, Taylor, or Reid cases, and a child who was ten at that time would be more than sixty years old today. So it is reasonable to assume that scarcely anyone under sixty knows what the author of that history is talking about. What *was* the Arbuckle rape case? Why wasn't the William Desmond Taylor murder solved—and why were two stars ostracized because of it? How did Wallace Reid become a junkie?

Rex Harrison and wife Lilli Palmer felt the heat of scandal when Carole Landis killed herself in 1948. Carole took sleeping pills because "Sexy Rexy" didn't return her love.   *Los Angeles Examiner*

These are reasonable questions that may properly be asked by anyone who reads a history of motion pictures. The same may be said of other famous Hollywood scandals. A person who was ten on the day that Ingrid Bergman, married to a man in Hollywood, bore a baby to her lover in Rome would be thirty-six today. The under-thirty-six group must often wonder what all the fuss over Bergman was all about.

These are chapters missing from almost any history of Hollywood. The suggestion is that there is something not quite nice about recalling such scandals. They are better left forgotten, some say. But are they right?

I don't think so. A historian of the 21st century, surveying the United States—indeed, the Western world—in the 20th century, will be more concerned with Errol Flynn's light-hearted peccadilloes than with the anamorphic lens. To get a true picture of life in 17th-century England, we turn to Samuel Pepys, whose diary presents an uncensored account of a townsman's days. In the 18th century we find the most revealing view in the pages of James Boswell's journals. Elizabeth Jenkins, in her superb biography, *Elizabeth the Great,* probes deeply into the sexual appetites and activities of "the Virgin Queen." Her reward, very properly, is high praise from the academic historian, Dr. A.L. Rowse: "This book gets nearer to penetrating the secret of the most remarkable woman in history than anyone has ever done. . . . Quite the most perceptive book about Elizabeth I that I have ever read." But if Good Queen Bess were a contemporary, Elizabeth Jenkins would have been discouraged from writing about the scandals that touched that monarch's life. Even the sex life of Queen Victoria—*after* Albert's death—has become part of the subject matter of a book; presumably that ostensibly unshakable keystone of 19th-century priggery has been dead long enough to make her true life fit to print (if anyone can find out the facts at this late date).

The professed disdain for scandalous information is so much nonsense, of course. We are all interested in scandal because it is the common denominator of mankind. Indeed, the Bible equates scandal with knowledge itself in the story of Adam and Eve, who ate the forbidden fruit of "the tree of the knowledge of good and evil," after which "the eyes of them both were opened, and they knew that they were naked." And scandal has been with us ever since. If we do not ourselves become involved in scandal, it is not because we are incapa-

Clara Bow, whom Elinor Glyn dubbed the "It" girl. Among the men who frequented her Chinese den were Gary Cooper, John Wayne, and a physician whose wife sued the flapper for alienation of affections.

The Museum of Modern Art/Film Stills Archive

ble of it, but because a few of us are more susceptible to some human frailties than others. One man (or woman—there is no discrimination in such matters) will kick over the traces of respectability sexually, while another commits the sin of pride, and still a third gives in completely to the spirit of covetousness. We are all sinners, and it ill behooves any of us to look sanctimoniously on those who get caught in sin.

In other words, although this book is about scandals, it is not written with the intention of holding unfortunate persons up to public shame or embarrassment anew. It is, rather, sympathetic to the principals in these scandals. It is to be hoped that a calm view of these scandals will show the public the injustice and cruelty of leaping to conclusions and hounding the unfortunate. *Let him who is without sin cast the first stone,* as Holy Writ says. Ingrid Bergman has little reason to look back with self-reproach on the most tempestuous event of her life, a time of crisis through which she passed with dignity, like the noble woman she is. But the millions who condemned her in her time of trouble—the self-righteous who presumed to set themselves up, like the Almighty Himself, to judge her—may well recall that time with shame.

We can all rejoice at the change in public opinion in recent years, a change which has put an end to talk of barring from the screen those stars who may be involved in scandals. In the past decade, unwed actresses have been able to freely acknowledge their pregnancies, actors and actresses have lived together openly, and most people have shown a willingness to face up to the fact that weaknesses of the flesh are common to all of us. This is as it should be: if we are able to enjoy the pleasant things of life vicariously through the stars, let us not desert them when they are afflicted with misfortune.

There were scandals in the film world before there were movie stars. Indeed, it may be said that Hollywood scandals antedated Hollywood itself.

One of the pioneers in motion pictures was an Englishman, Eadweard Muybridge, who first took motion pictures of a galloping horse in 1877. Muybridge was in California working on a geodetic survey for the U.S. government at the time that Governor Leland Stanford made a historic bet with two other horse racing enthusiasts, James R. Keene and Frederick MacCrellish. Stanford wagered $25,000 that a horse sometimes has all four hooves off the ground when galloping.

The difficulty was how to settle the argument. Photography, then in a somewhat primitive state, seemed to be the most logical answer. Muybridge solved the problem by lining up twenty-four cameras to take pictures one after another. The photos proved Stanford was right.

Muybridge's multi-camera setup was a direct precursor of the motion picture camera. His personal life was a portent of what lay ahead for the movies. Muybridge's real name was Edward James Muggeridge. Two years after the galloping horse feat, Muybridge began to suspect that a U.S. Army major was cuckolding him. Muybridge went to the officer's house one night, stood outside in the darkness, and called for his wife's lover to come out. When the major stepped through the door, Muybridge cried out, "Here is a message from my wife," and shot the fellow through the heart. A jury at Napa, California, acquitted Muybridge after he invoked the then popular "unwritten law."

When motion pictures became a popular entertainment, they were free of scandal at first, for a very good reason—the actors and actresses in such dramas as *The Great Train Robbery, Her Newsboy Friend,* and *A True Indian's Heart* were not identified. The anonymity of film actors in the early days resulted from the reluctance of actors to be identified with such a disreputable medium (movies were still frowned upon by genteel folk) and from the desire of the producers to keep wages low. In fact, the low level of actors' pay in the early days was itself a major reason for the lack of scandal. Sin, like most of the other pleasures of life, thrives where there is an ample supply of money; virtue most often exists among those who cannot afford vice. And in those days movie actors could scarcely afford even virtue. Between 1896 and 1910, when movies began to be shown publicly, film actors were generally paid between $5 and $15 a day.

But nickelodeon fans, in a storm of letters to the producers, were demanding to know the names of the actors and actresses they had come to recognize in film after film. The film trust—an apparently impregnable monopoly headed by Thomas A. Edison and nine producers—ignored the letters. But Carl Laemmle, who was one of the independents struggling to break the power of the film trust, saw in them a way to strike a blow for his own cause. He hired Florence Lawrence, who had been billed before simply as "The Biograph Girl" (Biograph being a major movie studio) and publicized her by name as his own star. The other independents followed suit and soon the film trust had no alternative but to do the same.

The effect on actors' salaries was breathtaking. By 1914 the stars were making from $250 to $2,000 a week and the pay of supporting actors had soared proportionately. The actors overnight had become the most important element in film-making. They could virtually name their own figures. Mary Pickford was one of the stars who did just that. After she had been working for Adolph Zukor for two years and had demonstrated her value as a box-office drawing card, she went to Zukor and said, "Mr. Zukor, for years I've dreamed of making twenty thousand dollars a year before I was twenty. And I'll be twenty very soon now." She got the twenty thousand, then raised the ante to one hundred thousand a year, then to half a million (this in an era when there was little or no tax on incomes). Finally Miss Pickford was making nearly a million dollars a year, including 50 percent of the profits on her pictures, when she decided to join with her then husband, Douglas Fairbanks, Charles Chaplin, and producer David Wark Griffith in forming United Artists Corporation, so that they could keep *all* the profits from their pictures.

Mary Pickford didn't let her newly found riches go to her head, nor did many other actors, actresses, producers, and directors. But there were many who found all that money so overwhelming that they completely lost all sense of perspective. As the *New York Journal's* Hollywood correspondent put it at the time, "When people spring from poverty to affluence within a few weeks, their mental equipment is not always equal to the strain. They have money, an unaccustomed toy, and they spend it in bizarre ways. They may indulge in 'wild parties' or they may indulge in other forms of relaxation and excitement. Many of them spend all they make. Since Prohibition came in, many of them who had no liquor stocks turned to other stimulants. The dealers in illicit drugs found a growing market." Only a "relatively small group" in Hollywood went in for this sort of thing, the correspondent added.

Almost every visitor to Hollywood in the postwar decade made the same observation. The British novelist, Elinor Glyn, who helped usher in the new ways of the Roaring Twenties, told the *New York Times,* "The trouble with the movie industry is that so many young people in it get rich suddenly. They are not taught control and it is hard for them to resist temptation. A young girl acts with a handsome young star all day in emotional scenes, and when she gets through she is apt to think that her husband is an awful bore."

Perhaps in New York, with its sophistication, its theatrical traditions, and its countless leisure-time resources, the newly rich actors might have managed to handle themselves without too much nastiness. But in 1908 the trek to Hollywood had begun. The moviemakers went West for two reasons: they could depend on year-round sunlight for their cameras, and they were far from the film trust and close to the Mexican border, close enough to make a quick getaway, if need be. The independents had good reason to think in those terms; when the film trust—which was not broken by court order until 1917—cracked down, it played rough. The independents were raided by goons from the film trust who wielded brass knuckles and iron pipes. Cameras and film were seized. Even in Hollywood, Cecil B. DeMille used to wear a pistol and carry the day's takes home with him every night for safekeeping, and one night he was shot at. If the film trust chose to fight in the courts by getting an injunction, an independent producer could slip across the border into Mexico and continue his work.

Sometimes the movie people slipped across the border for other reasons. Mack Sennett once rushed his entire troupe into Mexico after he got a tip that a seventeen-year-old girl who had generously bestowed her favors on virtually every able-bodied man in the film colony, had gone to the district attorney with a statutory rape complaint. Weeks later, the Sennett group was able to return to Hollywood; the girl, unaccountably, had named a Santa Barbara grocer, not an actor (or actors).

When the movie people moved in, Vine Street was a deeply rutted dirt road with a row of pepper trees down the middle. Barns were rented as studios. Coyotes howled in Cahuenga Canyon. Informality was the style: movie queens could be seen, coats flung over their nightgowns, getting bottles of milk and newspapers at the drug stores (or store—in the beginning there was just one).

In 1910 Hollywood had been annexed by Los Angeles, but it was still eight miles out in the country and people used to go to the Hollywood Hotel as a rural retreat. There were dances on Thursday nights, with all the top stars in attendance, and many of the stars lived in the hotel. A step down the ladder was the Alexandria Hotel; five o'clock was casting time at the

When Olive Thomas took poison in a Paris hotel, Selznick Pictures lost a star and Jack Pickford a bride. Rumors of drug addiction put Sin City on the defensive.

Eddie Brandt's
Saturday Matinee

A violinist plays music for Wally Reid to emote by. Wally died at thirty, a drug addict and one of the first victims of the star system.

The Museum of Modern Art/Film Stills Archive

bar there. Actors who needed work could also put up their photos on the wall of a Hollywood grocery store.

Flamboyance was the fashion. Nazimova shocked all Los Angeles by strolling along Sunset Boulevard in bright yellow pajamas in broad daylight, in a period when pajamas were strictly for bedroom wear. Bebe Daniels got ten days in jail for going seventy-five miles an hour in her powerful car down a dirt road in Santa Ana, but Abe Lyman brought his band to serenade her and a restaurant sent in special meals and advertised, "We are feeding Bebe Daniels." Some of the cowboy extras from the horse operas liked to have fun occasionally firing their pistols in the streets, a sport that unnerved many Angelenos, especially when they learned that the pistols often had live ammunition. (One Japanese gardener got so annoyed that he got a pistol himself and shot director Francis Boggs to death at the Selig studio near Eighth and Hill Streets.)

The people who had lived in Los Angeles, and especially in Hollywood before the invasion of the movie folk, didn't like it at all. They put up signs, "No Dogs or Actors," which irritated dog fanciers no end. The actors were unwelcome in local organizations; even William DeMille, whose background and breeding should have made him acceptable anywhere, was barred from the Los Angeles Country Club. (Only one actor has ever been accepted as a member by the Los Angeles Country Club—Harold Lloyd, long after his career in motion pictures was over, when he was engaged in investment management and real estate development.)

That attitude, to a considerable degree, has persisted over the years. The Angelenos didn't care that Gloria Swanson bathed in a solid gold tub sunk into the floor of a black marble bathroom. They were indifferent to the fourteen-carat gold ceiling of Marion Davies' living room. It was unimportant to them that Mary Pickford's mansion, "Pickfair," was one of the most palatial establishments in the entire country. They scoffed at reports that Valentino had nothing but black walls in "Falcon's Lair," his famous mountain-top home.

The Angelenos *did* know that Tom Mix had put up his initials in a huge electrical sign over his Beverly Hills mansion. They didn't like it.

The attitude of the local people was a clue to the way the whole nation would react when there was trouble. Unrecognized by Hollywood, a feeling of hostility toward the stars was growing throughout America. As Benjamin B. Hampton, writing in 1931, just a decade later, said, "For several years the stories of huge wages were regarded as showman exaggerations, merely the reckless boasting of inspired press agents. People thought it preposterous that a girl, unknown a year or two earlier, should be receiving $2,000 a week, or that a plumber's assistant should have become a comedian worth a quarter of a million a year. But gradually theater patrons came to realize that these stories were true, and realization was accompanied by mixed emotions that in many instances turned to bitterness and hostility. Admiration and adoration of movie celebrities had developed without any very sound basis, and now many people who had formed the habit of idolizing their favorites as superior beings were shocked to discover that their divinities were money-grubbers of the most ordinary variety. Merchants and professional men, struggling to earn five or ten thousand dollars a year, began to curse the 'pretty boys' of the screen who received as much in a month or a week, and their wives grew caustic in commenting on the 'dough-faced girls who hadn't brains enough to act, but were lucky enough to get a fortune for being clotheshorses.' "

The newspaper stories out of Hollywood had been hinting, more and more, at some of the less innocuous aspects of life in the new film capital. The phrase "casting couch" came into common use throughout the country. Rumors of orgies, brothels, and studio call girls swept across the continent. Articles about narcotics, blackmail, and divorce were appearing in the press every day; even divorce was only condoned by a small segment of the population at that time.

Of course, none of these things was unique to Hollywood. It was the beginning of the Roaring Twenties, the immediate postwar era, the Aspirin Age, the debut of the flappers, the time of Prohibition. Moral standards were changing everywhere, not just in Hollywood. There was a new sexual freedom. The old order was being overturned in every hamlet of America.

But the changes were not immediately apparent in, say, Albany, New York; or Peoria, Illinois; or Arlington, Minnesota; or Tucson, Arizona; or Oshawa, Ontario.

Hollywood, on the other hand, was living in a glass house. Many Americans didn't like what they saw going on there. The stage was set for trouble—and the cameras were ready to start rolling.

2 Roscoe (Fatty) Arbuckle:
A Party in 'Frisco

As the summer of 1921 drew to an end, Roscoe Arbuckle was able to reflect that he was sitting on top of the world. He had just signed a contract that would pay him three million dollars over a three-year period, or almost three thousand dollars a day.

Called "Fatty" by millions of moviegoers but never anything but "Roscoe" by his friends, Arbuckle was one of the greatest comedy stars of his time. He was perhaps the most popular star of all as far as the children of the world were concerned, and only those who felt that anything projected on the silver screen had to be evil excluded themselves from his following.

It is surely one of the classic ironies in the history of puritanism in the United States that the first big scandal involving that instrument of the Devil, motion pictures, should involve an actor whose films had been notably free of anything objectionable.

As the Labor Day weekend approached, Arbuckle finished the last of three consecutive feature pictures—without a day off in between them—for Famous Players-Lasky, the studio

After a Prohibition drinking party at the St. Francis, starlet Virginia Rappe died of a ruptured bladder. Fatty Arbuckle was accused of rape and charged with murder. *Eddie Brandt's Saturday Matinee*

that later became Paramount Pictures. Arbuckle felt the need of some boisterous relaxation. But Los Angeles was too familiar and too much of a small town in those days, a dull little place; all the fun was in cosmopolitan, tolerant San Francisco.

So Arbuckle took off from Hollywood with a couple of friends in his twenty-five-thousand-dollar Rolls Royce. It was a journey to oblivion, a trip that would bring death to a young woman, ruin to his career, and unexpected perils to the entire industry which had enriched him.

Roscoe Arbuckle was born in Smith Corners, Kansas, on March 24, 1887. He was just thirty-four when the death of Virginia Rappe, after a party in his San Francisco hotel room, brought his career to an end.

In that short span, however, he played a not inconsiderable part in nurturing motion pictures through their uncertain infancy. He represented an era, but the cliché that "his death marked the end of an era" could not be said of him. He died professionally a decade before he passed away in the flesh, but that decade in Hollywood proved that his downfall had brought about no significant change in the new order which was fast becoming the old order.

Roscoe was still an infant when his parents moved from the Midwest to California, which made him one of the few early film stars who had grown up on the West Coast. He was only eight years old when he first appeared on the stage before an audience in San Jose, California, with the stock company of Frank Bacon. Arbuckle spent his youth in Southern California.

There is nothing to indicate that Arbuckle ever spent much time in school. Whatever education he had he picked up backstage from the older actors, actresses, and stagehands. He spent his entire boyhood backstage; all he cared about was show business, and he did anything and everything he could to remain in that exciting field. He was fat from the time he learned to walk, and this limited his opportunity. Nevertheless, he managed to find work somehow. As a boy he worked as ticket-taker; at seventeen he was singing "illustrated songs" in a San Jose nickelodeon; and finally Leon Errol, later a well-known comedian in the movies but then manager of the Orpheum Theater in Portland, Oregon, let him go onstage with his own vaudeville act, a blackface monologist in the heyday of blackface acts.

He must have won a certain amount of popularity, for in

1905 Murads cigarettes ran an advertisement carrying his endorsement—the first cigarette testimonial in what was to become a long and absurd chapter in the history of advertising.

In 1913 Mack Sennett gave the young entertainer a tryout for his two-reel comedies. Arbuckle must have been doing badly in vaudeville at the time, for he accepted Sennett's offer of a job as one of the Keystone Cops at the magnificent salary of three dollars a day.

Within a short time, however, Arbuckle was to appear on a list of the most highly paid stars of show business, as published in *Variety,* the show business trade journal. Arbuckle was making $1,250 a week then, which put him in a tie for eighth place with Elbert Hubbard, the homespun "philosopher," behind Gertrude Hoffman, Eva Tanguay, hypnotist J. Robert Pauline, swimmer and film star Annette Kellerman, female impersonator Julian Eltinge, Alice Lloyd, and the Gus Edwards Song Revue, but well ahead of such famous entertainers as Lionel Barrymore and Pat Rooney.

But Arbuckle's four-figure weekly income did not begin until he had graduated from the Keystone Cops comedies. He emerged as a star in his own two-reelers for Sennett, appearing with other Keystone stars including Charlie Chaplin and Mabel Normand (both of whom would also be involved in scandals eventually).

Sennett used to advertise his comedies as "The Great Big Splashes of Fun and Beauty," and it was honest advertising: slapstick humor and pretty girls made an unbeatable combination. Sennett discovered great talents and gave them considerable liberty in developing their own brand of humor, and much of his best film resulted from the spontaneous horseplay and high spirits of his troupe.

In 1917 Arbuckle left Sennett to make his own comedies for Famous Players-Lasky, but a few months later Sennett himself was in the FPL setup, having moved his entire operation into that rapidly expanding organization. Joseph M. Schenck was then a producer at the studio, and he and Arbuckle became friends. In the light of the widespread belief that there are no loyalties in Hollywood, it is worth noting that they remained friends, even after Arbuckle's personal disaster cost Schenck millions of dollars. Indeed, most of Hollywood, like Schenck, remained steadfast in Arbuckle's defense until the end—perhaps too steadfast.

The FPL Colony Studios on East Forty-eighth Street in New

York housed Arbuckle's comedy company in the beginning. But he was there less than a year. Then FPL decided to move almost all its operations out to Hollywood, including Arbuckle's group. Most of the other movie makers were already on the West Coast. Arbuckle was now one of the most highly paid men in the movies or in any other industry; nobody in pictures was a bigger attraction except Charlie Chaplin.

As Gene Fowler once rhapsodized in an adjective-strewn panegyric, all other pie-throwing comedians "were mere petit fours twiddlers when compared with that greatest custard slinger of all time, the mightiest triple-threat man that ever stepped on the waffle-iron, the All-American of All-Americans, the supreme grand lama of the meringue, the Hercules of the winged dessert, the Ajax of the hurtling fritter, the paragon of patty-casters, the unconquerable and valiant flinger of open and closed mince models, the monarch of the zooming rissoles . . . Roscoe (Fatty) Arbuckle!"

Everybody loved Fatty Arbuckle—even other actors—and Arbuckle loved the world. He appeared to be as jolly as fat men are supposed to be. A down-at-the-heels variety act could always depend on the open-handed star for a grubstake and a word of encouragement, and he gave advice as freely as he gave money. His advice was valuable, too, for he knew his craft thoroughly. Unlettered he might be, but stupid he was not; he had an active, intelligent mind and his on-screen madness had method to it. He knew what he was doing every second that he was on the screen.

Off the screen the same could not be said of him. He was too often a puppet dancing to strings pulled by his own passions and emotions, capable of doing things contrary to prudence and common sense. In the light of what later transpired, it is worth pausing to consider Buster Keaton's appraisal of his old and dear friend in his autobiography, *My Wonderful World of Slapstick*. Arbuckle, he recalled, "had no meanness, malice or jealousy in him."

This was Roscoe (Fatty) Arbuckle at the top of the heap, soon to be at the bottom; the most beloved actor of millions of Americans, soon to be despised.

A kindly Providence gave Arbuckle warning. Three years before disaster overcame him, an orgy in Boston (of all places!) almost erupted into a public scandal. It should have been a hint to him that this sort of thing was highly dangerous for a public figure, one of the biggest stars in Hollywood, but it didn't.

The orgy that Boston newspapermen later came to call the "hundred-thousand-dollar girl and champagne party" began soberly enough. Arbuckle was making a brief personal appearance in Boston, and a great banquet was held in his honor. The dinner, attended by a score of national leaders in the industry, was held in the Copley Plaza, a conservative Back Bay hotel. Before midnight the party broke up, but most of the men present were bundled into touring cars and driven off to Brownie Kennedy's roadhouse at Mishawum Manor, outside Boston at Woburn. They had called ahead, and by the time they got there the roadhouse was all lit up and rarin' to go, and so were the girls inside it.

The booze was good and the girls were not, and the orgy was a rousing success, as such things go.

Unfortunately, however, there had to come a morning after. In this case, came the dawn and two of the girls began to mutter that they'd been had. They later told the authorities they had been engaged to perform as "professional musicians," ignoring the ribald grins that greeted their statement, and had been promised fifty dollars for their endeavors. But the woman who operated the roadhouse refused to pay them the next day, for some reason, perhaps because they had tried to earn their pay by playing music instead of games. The girls threatened to go to the police, but the resort keeper said she wasn't afraid of that, because the authorities had been paid off to overlook her establishment.

The two girls were still angry. So they complained to the district attorney, and he looked into the whole affair.

What happened after that became a matter of dispute and inquiry by several official bodies. One thing is known: less than a month after their frolic at Brownie Kennedy's, the host of the party got word that some of the girls were talking about their erstwhile playmates. He hastily summoned the industry bosses to a secret gathering, not for fun, at New London, Connecticut, not far from Boston (or from Long Island Sound, if any of the men cared to throw themselves in), but safely outside the legal jurisdiction of Massachusetts. The grim-faced men decided to put up a war chest of one hundred thousand dollars, to be used as their man on the spot deemed advisable.

Where did the money go? That has never been established definitely.

The wild party at Brownie Kennedy's took place in the early morning hours of March 7, 1917. On July 21, 1921, Attorney

General Allen charged that there was a connection between the DA's office and the suppression of the scandal. The attorney general alleged that there were threats to prosecute the motion picture producers, actors, and theater owners who had attended the orgy; that a lawyer then extorted one hundred thousand dollars from the men; and that no action was taken against them. Arbuckle was named by the attorney general as one of those who had enjoyed the hospitality of Brownie Kennedy's cozy cottage—an allegation denied by those who were, unquestionably, present—but the newspapers were kind to him then. His part, if any, in the proceedings was soft-pedaled and it didn't hurt his career at all.

Another man might have been chastened by such a narrow brush with scandal; not Arbuckle. His life went on, unshadowed by evil omens, for six more months, until the scandal that was to destroy him burst upon him.

Calamity seemed far away from Arbuckle and his crowd. Most of them in their twenties and full of spirit, they had more money than they had ever expected to see, and the world idolized them. It was a heady experience, somewhat akin to the sudden freedom that many a youth discovers for the first time when he goes away to college.

But this was complete freedom, not the limited freedom of a campus. These young people, most of them of little education, had known poverty and deprivation as children, and now they were determined to catch up belatedly on the pleasant things of life. They loved carefree horseplay and went in for so many practical jokes that before long they were barred from half the lots in Hollywood. They drank far too much, as thousands of other American young people were doing in those frenetic days of the Noble Experiment. They explored sex with the enthusiasm and the vigor of alley cats.

There were always plenty of willing girls, hopeful that a horizontal encounter with an actor might lead to a vertical career before the cameras; they were usually disappointed, often in more ways than one. Girls flocked from all over the country to Hollywood. What they found there depended to a large extent on Luck, and like most ladies, Luck rarely looked with a kind eye on other women.

Among the girls who turned up in Hollywood was Virginia Rappe. She was twenty when she arrived there, five years before her death. She had been a model of sorts and best known for the fact that her picture appeared on the sheet

Arbuckle with Mabel Normand in *When Comedy Was King*. Mabel had more than her share of troubles—with Mack Sennett, with William Desmond Taylor, with drugs, and with the big C.   *Freda Keefer Collection*

music for the song, "Let Me Call You Sweetheart." In Hollywood she got a few bit parts in some two-reel comedies.

The photographs of her that survive show a brunette who is not noticeably pretty; she has a big look about her, although she was only five feet seven inches tall and weighed just one hundred and thirty-five pounds. Buster Keaton was an Arbuckle partisan, but his comment about her is nevertheless worth repeating: "She was about as virtuous as most of the other untalented young women who had been knocking around Hollywood for years, picking up small parts any way they could."

At the beginning of the Labor Day weekend in 1921, Virginia Rappe went to San Francisco. Why she went there was never made clear. She may have known that Arbuckle was going to be there.

On Sunday, the day before Labor Day, Arbuckle and two friends, actor Lowell Sherman and director Fred Fischbach, motored up to the northern California city. They checked into a three-room suite on the twelfth floor of the St. Francis Hotel. A case of whiskey and another of gin arrived, ice was sent up, people began arriving, and soon a party was well under way to the occasional but loud music of a phonograph that was wound up by anyone who happened to be near enough—and sober enough—to crank it.

People came and went all day, so it's impossible to pin down precisely who was there. In addition to Arbuckle, Fischbach, and Lowell, it's known that three showgirls were there, and there were certainly others. In due course Virginia Rappe arrived, in response to a telephoned summons from Arbuckle, and with her she thoughtfully brought her agent and a friend.

What happened after that is still unclear, despite public testimony and presentation of evidence at the inquest, the preliminary hearing, and the three trials of Roscoe Arbuckle. There were charges and counter-charges of bribery, perjury, suppression of evidence, intimidation, coaching of witnesses.

At that time there were persons in the state government who had a few scores to settle with the movie industry, and apparently hoped to settle them in the course of Arbuckle's prosecution. There were men prominent in the movie industry who would stop at almost nothing to protect their industry and their properties.

Both sides saw issues in the case greater than the fate of

Virginia Rappe or even of Fatty Arbuckle. That explains the record of the hearings with key witnesses changing their stories or disappearing altogether. The result is that no one, in all probability, will ever know the truth about what happened in the St. Francis Hotel that day.

According to all accounts, Virginia Rappe appeared to be in the best of health when she arrived at the party. There was little need to search for the room number; the sounds of revelry, scratching records, deep bellows of masculine laughter, feminine giggles, the tinkle of bottles against glasses could be heard far down the hall.

At some point in the proceedings, Virginia Rappe became ill. She was taken to another room in the hotel and treated there by the house physician until Wednesday. Then she was removed to a private nursing home, where she died the next day. The attending physicians, puzzled, performed an autopsy but signed the death certificate.

That would normally have closed the case, as far as the authorities were concerned. It would appear to be a natural death not requiring investigation. Virginia Rappe might have gone to her death an obscure bit player, known only to other film actors, and Fatty Arbuckle might have gone on indefinitely amusing audiences the world over by his innocent antics had not a woman on the hospital staff become curious.

She telephoned the coroner's office and asked Deputy Coroner Michael Brown when the autopsy was to be performed. "What autopsy are you talking about?" Dr. Brown asked. He had received no report of an unusual death. Before the woman could answer, he heard another voice in the background whispering to her; she gasped and hung up.

His curiosity now fully aroused, Dr. Brown telephoned the hospital and recognized the voice that answered as that of his caller. When he began to question her, however, she denied her identity and said, "I'm sorry, I have no information to give you."

That did it. Dr. Brown went to the hospital and began an investigation. He learned the name of the woman who had died there. He examined her body in the morgue. He saw that the bladder was ruptured. It didn't look like a natural death to him.

He called the police.

The police reporters for the San Francisco newspapers got wind of the story. Almost instantly it flashed across the news service wires to New York, where it became the banner line on Page One:

Fatty Arbuckle Sought in Orgy Death!

Even before the inquest was held, there was an omen of what lay ahead. Harry Kelly, secretary of the grand jury, issued a statement in which he said, "So many women's clubs and private individuals interested in the moral welfare of the city have demanded an investigation that I will present their demands to the jury. It is our duty to investigate such things, and we will certainly do so."

The day before the inquest, Hearst's *New York American* ran a screamer headline:

Arbuckle Held in Jail on Charge of Murder.

The front page headline the next day, September 13, was even better for circulation:

Inquest Bares Full Story of Arbuckle Orgy.

Arbuckle gave the press a statement embodying his version of the affair. It told of his arrival in San Francisco the day after Miss Rappe and her two friends had arrived there. Then it went on:

"At my invitation they came to my rooms to have a few drinks. I was clad in pajamas, bathrobe, and bedroom slippers, and was having my breakfast when the trio entered. We sat in the room, had a few drinks, and talked over matters that concerned us.

"Shortly after Miss Rappe had taken a few drinks she became hysterical, complained that she could not breathe, and then started to tear off her clothes. I requested two girls present at the time to take care of Miss Rappe. She was disrobed and placed in a bath tub to be revived. The immersion did not benefit her, and I then telephoned to the hotel manager, telling him what was wrong, and requested that Miss Rappe be given a room. She was taken out of my room and put to bed.

"When no change came in Miss Rappe's condition, I summoned a physician. I departed from the St. Francis Tuesday (September 6), having engaged passage on the steamer *Harvard* the Saturday before to go to Los Angeles. The report that I was ordered by the management to leave the St. Francis is not true.

"I was at no time alone with Miss Rappe. During the time in my rooms there were at least half a dozen people there all the time and I can produce witnesses to bear out that statement. I am only too glad to return to San Francisco to assist the authorities in straightening out this horrible mess."

It was a pallid statement, apparently calculated to diminish interest in the case. But if that was the hope, it was sadly misplaced. For Mrs. Bambina Maude Delmont, Virginia Rappe's friend, stepped forward with her story in the form of an affidavit to the police, and it was a good deal spicier.

She said that Virginia had two or three drinks after they arrived at the party. Then, Arbuckle suddenly shoved Virginia into an adjoining bedroom, locking the door. As he did it, Mrs. Delmont recalled, he told the girl, "I've waited for you five years, and now I've got you," as corny as the titles that used to appear on the silent film melodramas.

While this was going on, Mrs. Delmont did nothing. As she explained, "I did not know Miss Rappe too well, so I did not want to interfere." Presumably she thought this sort of thing might be an every-day occurrence with the Arbuckle-Rappe crowd.

Then Mrs. Delmont began to hear Miss Rappe screaming. The screams did not sound commonplace; they sounded as though Miss Rappe were desperately in earnest. The screams continued from room 1219 although Mrs. Delmont, now thoroughly alarmed, kicked and pounded at the door. After a half hour, she said, she grabbed the telephone and called to the hotel desk for help. Assistant Manager H. J. Boyle was sent up to the room.

Just as Boyle arrived, Arbuckle opened the door to 1219 and came out in his pajamas, wearing Virginia Rappe's hat tilted jauntily atop his head and his familiar "foolish screen smile," as Mrs. Delmont later described it, on his face.

"Go in and get her dressed and take her back to the Palace," Arbuckle told Mrs. Delmont, according to her account. "She makes too much noise."

The women in the party slipped into room 1219 and found the Rappe girl virtually nude. Her clothes—a green jersey jacket, a matching skirt, a white silk teddy trimmed with green (a teddy was a woman's one-piece undergarment of the time, consisting of a top combined with loose-fitting drawers), a white silk waist, and a pair of black lace garters—had been torn off her and lay strewn about the floor. Virginia was sobbing with the pain that tore at her insides.

"I'm dying," she moaned to Mrs. Delmont. "I'm dying, I'm dying. Arbuckle did it. He hurt me."

Arbuckle snorted. He told the others that the girl wasn't hurt, she was just "putting it on." He told her to shut up or he'd throw her out of the window.

What had been done to Virginia Rappe in room 1219 while the door was locked? That was what the public was waiting to be told. The public remained frustrated for several days, until the preliminary hearing. Then Al Seminacher told the court what Arbuckle himself had said about the activities in the locked room.

Seminacher said that on the day after the party, three days before Miss Rappe died, Arbuckle, Sherman, Fischbach, Arbuckle's chauffeur, Harry McCullough, and Seminacher were together in Arbuckle's suite at the St. Francis when Arbuckle began to give them a detailed account of his sex adventure with her. He told them, or so Seminacher said, that he had shoved a big piece of ice into her genitals. "Everyone laughed," Seminacher recalled.

Seminacher had been called to the stand at the police court hearing as a defense witness. His testimony was a real blow to the defense. A New York reporter covering the trial wrote: "Details of the assault were whispered to the court reporter, written on a bit of paper, and passed around among the attorneys." This unusual procedure took place after Seminacher, ordered to give the details that Arbuckle had told his friends, objected to testifying to them in public.

The case was getting worse for Arbuckle. The coroner's jury had already decided that he was criminally responsible for the girl's death. Demanding that Arbuckle be prosecuted for manslaughter, the coroner's jury called on the authorities to "take steps to prevent a further occurrence of such events, so that San Francisco will not be made the rendezvous of the debauchee and the gangster."

The language was getting rougher. It reflected public opinion, which was rising swiftly against Arbuckle.

Public sentiment was whipped up still more by Henry Lehrman, a director and producer for Selznick, who had, it seemed, been Rappe's fiancé at the time of her unfortunate

Virginia Rappe. "She was about as virtuous as most of the other untalented women who had been knocking around Hollywood for years, picking up small parts any way they could," said Buster Keaton.

Eddie Brandt's Saturday Matinee

demise. Lehrman, Vienna-born, directed Chaplin in his first pictures. Known to his friends as "Pathe" because he had bluffed his way into movies by pretending to represent the Pathe Company of France, Lehrman had been a friend of Arbuckle for a decade.

After Miss Rappe's death, Lehrman publicly and frequently proclaimed his unshaken belief in his intended's virtue and in Arbuckle's perfidy. Lehrman had been in New York when Miss Rappe died, and he said he had been "advised"—he didn't say by whom—to remain there. So he summoned the press to tell them that he had sent a thousand dollars' worth of tiger lilies to cover her coffin. (Some eight thousand persons filed past her bier in a Los Angeles undertaking establishment.)

Unlike most movie folk, especially those who thought that Arbuckle might, indeed, be guilty, Lehrman was eager to tell the world what he thought, in order to clear the fair name of his fiancée.

"My prayer is that justice be done," Lehrman said. "I don't want to go to the Coast now. I could not face Arbuckle. I would kill him. If he wants to live, he had better be punished."

Lehrman fingered a pair of cufflinks that Miss Rappe had given him. They were inscribed: "To Henry, my first and last sacred love. Virginia."

"Virginia," Lehrman said, "had the most remarkable determination. She would rise from the dead to defend her person from indignity."

"I had a talk over the long distance telephone with Mrs. Sidi Spreckels. She said that before she knew she was going to die Virginia kept saying, 'Don't tell Henry! Don't tell Henry!' That means one thing: she had lost the battle she made to defend herself. She didn't want me to know her honor had been violated."

A more skeptical soul might have read another meaning into Miss Rappe's words, but nobody pointed that out to Lehrman.

Rape was an old story with Arbuckle, to hear Lehrman tell it. "He boasted to me that he had torn the clothing from an unwilling girl and outraged her," the director told a world that was just dying to be shocked. He said that Arbuckle had caused a great deal of difficulty because of his often unwelcome attentions to actresses. "I finally had to tell him that if he didn't keep out of the women's dressing rooms I would see that he was through," Lehrman added.

Miss Rappe had distrusted and disliked Arbuckle, Lehrman insisted in the face of the fact that she had gone to Arbuckle's suite in the hotel.

"Virginia always had a violent physical aversion to Arbuckle," he said. "When we three worked together I wanted everything to be like a happy family. One time when he attended a party her aversion sort of dampened things. I took her aside and said, 'Cheer up. Treat him pleasantly. He's a good fellow.' She replied, 'He's coarse and vulgar. He nauseates me. He is cheap and thinks he's funny.' "

With a showman's sure instinct for the dramatic, Lehrman painted his own picture of the fatal scene for the press:

"I can see now, in my mind's eye, how she must have fought him like a tiger, even if she had a couple of drinks. I remember once, when there was a terrible assault case in the newspapers, she said to me quietly, 'Henry, if anyone tried to do a thing like that to me, he'd have to kill me.' " Lehrman's shoulders sagged eloquently. "Well," he said, "she's dead."

It was great stuff, and the public ate it up. About the time of Arbuckle's first trial, however, the public learned that the grief-stricken fiancé had taken a "modiste's model" named Jocelyn Leigh to a smart Manhattan shop and bought her an expensive fur coat just a few days after Miss Rappe's death.

Throughout the country women's clubs, churches, reform groups, civic societies, and miscellaneous busybodies were loudly expressing their opinions. From Fresno to Falmouth, theater managers were being urged, implored, persuaded, or just plain ordered to stop showing Arbuckle films. (Films in which Miss Rappe appeared had been withdrawn as soon as she died.) In Geneva, a Danish delegate to an international conference even managed to drag poor Arbuckle's name into a discussion of white slavery.

"The smouldering gossip of corruption in the films broke into flame," Terry Ramsaye wrote five years later in his magnificent survey of the cinema, *A Million and One Nights.* "New York film offices were stricken with terror. There were endless conferences. Lawyers scurried about. Press agents tore at their hair and typewriters. Statements flew and the wires to San Francisco were overloaded. The set of facts was discouraging. It was difficult for even the most ingenious scenario makers to fit the admitted circumstances into an acceptable tale . . ."

The voices of sanity, justice, and fair play were few, and

they could scarcely be heard. But there were some. At the end of a long article reporting theaters and cities all over the country that had barred Arbuckle films, a New York newspaper carried a little item announcing that Fred G. Nixon-Nirdlinger, who controlled a string of Philadelphia theaters, intended to go on showing Arbuckle movies until and unless the fat man was convicted.

"There is no use kicking a man when he is down," said the brave theater owner. "Arbuckle has not been brought to trial yet, and until he is, cannot be called guilty, according to law. We can use our own judgment as to what happened, but until a legal decision is rendered, we should be fair to all concerned."

But nobody wanted to be fair. The storm had broken upon Hollywood and fate had chosen to sweep away the most vulnerable star of all, a fat man, and thus an easy object of revulsion. As famed attorney Earl Rogers, too tired and too sick to handle Arbuckle's defense, told Joe Schenck, "Arbuckle's weight will damn him. He will become a monster." A thin man might have done what Arbuckle did. But in fact, it wasn't a thin man; it was Fatty.

Responding to the fury of the mob, the state had obtained an indictment, not for manslaughter, as the coroner's jury had recommended, but for murder. The stated grounds for preferring this capital charge were that Arbuckle had caused Miss Rappe's death in the course of committing a felony (i.e., rape or attempted rape). However, no evidence was introduced at the trials to prove that Arbuckle committed rape or even attempted rape upon the person of Virginia Rappe.

Released on bail, Arbuckle returned to Los Angeles and received a mixed greeting. Inside the Santa Fe Railroad station more than a thousand friends in the industry, many of them stars, directors, and producers, had turned out to welcome him.

But outside another crowd was waiting, a crowd that represented most of the movie-going world. And the people in that crowd, when they saw Arbuckle, hissed and spat and called him "Murderer!" and "Big, fat slob!" and "Beast" and "Degenerate!"

In that dreadful moment the heart of Roscoe Arbuckle died. He would live for another decade or so, but he never again could be Fatty Arbuckle, the funny man. He had been shaken to the core. For the first time, he really comprehended the enormity of the misfortune that had befallen Virginia Rappe and Roscoe Arbuckle. He never forgot the horror and the pain of seeing hatred upon the faces of the people, the ordinary people who had adored him so recently. Even the tons of hate letters that he found awaiting him in Hollywood didn't affect him as much.

There were three trials in all. Both sides had elected to fight the case in the public prints, so an impartial trial was inconceivable. But the first trial ended in a hung jury, and so did the second. This reflected the courtroom genius of Frank Dominguez, the defense counsel, and the success of some film industry leaders in inducing key witnesses to vanish when they were needed.

Some of the testimony lived up to advance notices. There was Josephine Keza, a maid in the hotel, for example. She told of hearing "music, dancing, and doors slamming" from the room where Arbuckle's rowdy party was under way. Then, from the room next to it, she began to hear unbearable, heartbreaking screams. "When I heard the screams, I ran and listened," she said. Behind the door she heard a woman crying in pain, "No, no—oh, my God! No!" followed by Arbuckle's voice saying, "Shut up!" and then more screams. It apparently did not occur to the maid to notify the management about the odd goings-on on the twelfth floor.

Another witness gave testimony which indicated that Arbuckle had used ice in his sexual revels at least once before, a matter which surely must have intrigued any psychoanalysts who were following the case.

In defense of their friend, Arbuckle's adherents had been whispering that he had enjoyed Miss Rappe's favors on several previous occasions, so there would have been no reason for him to force himself upon her. But those rumors took a beating when Jesse K. Norgard took the witness stand for the prosecution. Norgard, janitor at a movie studio (one wonders how long he retained the job after testifying), swore that Arbuckle once offered him "a roll of bills" for a key to Miss Rappe's dressing room on the lot. The virtuous Norgard of course rejected the offer.

It was obvious that this testimony, if true, ruled out the possibility that Arbuckle had been Miss Rappe's lover. If he had been, he would scarcely have needed to bribe the janitor for a key to her room.

The defense did get in some telling blows. Dominguez managed to get the state's medical witnesses completely confused. Before they left the stand, they had been forced to admit that the peritonitis which killed Miss Rappe might not have been caused by anything that happened at the party. The peritonitis had resulted when her bladder was ruptured. It was the defense's contention that the shock of cold water, when the women at the party tried to revive Miss Rappe by immersing her in an icy tub, had ruptured the bladder.

The state, on the other hand, argued that Arbuckle's assault had caused the rupture. The mere weight of his body upon her in intercourse, when her bladder was distended from drinking, would have been enough to tear the bladder open, according to the prosecution.

The trials were lively affairs. One key defense witness was arrested for perjury a few hours after she testified that Miss Rappe had stayed at her resort to enjoy the company of men; the state was able to prove that Miss Rappe had not been away from home overnight at the time. The defense tried to get in its licks by calling as a witness an alleged fingerprint expert who was prepared to testify that Arbuckle's fingerprints, overlapping Miss Rappe's on the jamb of the door leading to his bedroom, as though she had clung to it until he pulled her hands away, had been forged. The judge decided that the witness was not qualified to testify as an expert.

The state was unable to use its best witness, Mrs. Delmont. The defense had investigated her background and discovered that she had committed bigamy. She later pleaded guilty to that charge and was released on probation, but her usefulness as a witness was over.

The press coverage was uninhibited throughout the trials. "Arbuckle Dragged Rappe Girl to Room, Woman Testifies," was a Page One headline in the usually restrained *New York Times.*

Some of the newspapers were ready to print anything that was lively and lurid regardless of its accuracy. One story, widely printed, had it that Miss Rappe was the bastard offspring of an English nobleman who had stayed in Chicago for a time, enjoying its famous hospitality, apparently.

Other articles pictured the obscure bit player (a "starlet" in today's parlance) as a famous actress, model, "and designer of women's clothes." One news service reporter wrote—with tongue in cheek, let us hope—that Miss Rappe "was reputed to have independent wealth as a result of oil investments.''

Three trials gave the newspapers ample time to grope about for new and wilder material when the courtroom drama itself began to pall, which didn't happen often. The papers loved the case; it sold more newspapers, one publisher disclosed, than anything since the Armistice.

The bitter clashes between opposing counsel furnished the papers with much printable material. (After the second trial Dominguez withdrew from the case and Gavin McNab became chief defense counsel.) One day the district attorney denounced ''this perjury and witness-bribing'' and McNab replied caustically by asking, ''When is he going to start in putting a stop to manufactured and perjured evidence?''

The first trial, in November 1921, ended in a mistrial when the jury persisted in a ten to two vote for acquittal. Of the five women on the jury, three had voted for acquittal and one, Mrs. Helen M. Hubbard, for conviction. The fifth had wavered; although she believed Arbuckle guilty and thought he should be convicted, she agreed after the first ballot to change her vote from ''guilty'' to ''not guilty.'' But Mrs. Hubbard clung to her ''guilty'' vote, and one male juror, who had wavered from side to side, finally settled down as a permanent ally of hers. After forty-one hours of deliberation, the jury was excused.

Then it was learned that Mrs. Hubbard and her family had received threats aimed at forcing her to change her vote. An official investigation was begun, but nothing ever came of it.

The second trial in January 1922 also ended in a mistrial when the jury again found itself ten to two for acquittal after forty-five hours.

Then came the third trial, which ended April 12, 1922.

It is worth noting, incidentally, that all three trials were held within seven months after Miss Rappe's death. This kind of speedy justice, guaranteed under the Constitution, seems to have become mostly a memory in our present-day courts. Today three such trials would take at least that many years, and by the time they were over nobody would really care very much about a dead girl named Virginia Rappe or a living man named Roscoe Arbuckle.

After the third jury heard the evidence, it took just six minutes to acquit Arbuckle. It did more than that: it expressed its regret for the ordeal he had undergone. ''Acquittal is not enough for Roscoe Arbuckle,'' the jury said. ''We feel a great injustice has been done him and there was not the slightest

Will Hays *(second from right)* hobnobbing with Irving Thalberg, Louis B. Mayer (inventor of the casting couch), and Harry Rapf.

The Museum of Modern Art/Film Stills Archive

Arbuckle directing under the pseudonym of William Goodrich. Has-beens come cheap in the dream factory. *The Museum of Modern Art/Film Stills Archive*

proof to connect him in any way with the commission of any crime." It read like a studio flack's press release rather than a verdict. But that's California.

The jury had exonerated Roscoe Arbuckle, but the public never forgave Fatty Arbuckle. The public agreed with Lehrman, who said, "This is what comes of taking vulgarians from the gutter and giving them enormous salaries and making idols of them. Some people don't know how to get a kick out of life, except in a beastly way. They are the ones who participate in orgies that surpass the orgies of degenerate Rome."

Lehrman also said, at the time of Arbuckle's arrest, "I want to live now to see that justice is not cheated. Nobody can pull me off. Arbuckle has powerful friends, and much influence and money will be used to save him. But he will have me to reckon with, even if he succeeds in buying his freedom."

But after Arbuckle's acquittal, nothing more was heard from Lehrman.

The three trials had cost Arbuckle more than one hundred thousand dollars, stripping him of his wealth, for he had never been a thrifty man. Indeed, Joe Schenck paid most of the legal fees. More importantly, the three trials cost Arbuckle his career.

Three Arbuckle films were "in the can," ready for release, when he was arrested. To this day they have never been shown publicly, and they probably never will be. And all of Arbuckle's earlier films were withdrawn from exhibition too.

Before the films were taken out of circulation, public officials all over the country took a holiday from civil liberties. Mayors and police chiefs everywhere were decreeing that no Arbuckle films were to be shown in their towns, although they had not the slightest legal justification for such high-handed actions. (They didn't charge that anything was wrong with the movies, just with the man who starred in them.) Who cared if such orders were unfair, unconstitutional, and unlawful; they were on the side of righteousness and morality, weren't they?

The theater owners and film distributors weren't disposed to argue with the self-appointed censors. After all, it was less than a decade since movies had become respectable.

But the uproar against Hollywood continued, and finally the studio bosses decided to follow the example of organized baseball, which had rehabilitated itself in the public's mind after the "Black Sox" World Series "fix" scandal by hiring Judge Kenesaw Mountain Landis as supreme arbiter.

The industry leaders knew just the man for their job. They had come to know him as chairman of the Republican National Committee during Warren G. Harding's successful bid for the Presidency the preceding year. He was now Postmaster General of the United States and an elder of the Presbyterian Church. He was forty-one-year-old William Harrison Hays. On December 8, 1921, the industry asked him to quit the government and become Hollywood's first "czar" at a salary of one hundred thousand dollars a year. On January 14, 1922, Will Hays, as he was usually called, accepted.

The ban on Arbuckle's films remained in effect by order of the Hays Office, as it came to be known, pending disposition of the charges against him. Hays took other actions designed to "clean up" Hollywood. He devised the "morality clause" which is still a part of contracts, posing a threat of contract cancellation over any actor who became involved in a scandal. He established the Central Casting Agency through which extras were hired, so that girls who went to Hollywood and turned to prostitution could be identified and barred from employment in the industry.

After Arbuckle's acquittal, Hays maintained a discreet silence for a few months and then suggested in a public statement that Arbuckle ought to be permitted to work in some capacity in the industry. "Every man in the right way and at the right time is entitled to his chance to make good," Hays said. "It is apparent that Roscoe Arbuckle's conduct since his trouble merits that chance. So far as I am concerned, there will be no suggestion now that he should not have his opportunity to go back to work in his own profession."

The groups that had denounced Arbuckle before rose up in wrath again at Hays's trial balloon. The New York State Federation of Churches, for example, passed a long-winded resolution charging that "to give Roscoe 'Fatty' Arbuckle another chance in motion pictures" would be to defy the parents of America and to condone "the capitalization of crime for financial gain," as well as to cripple efforts to "elevate the moral and artistic standards" of the motion picture industry.

That was how it went, through the length and breadth of the land. In Pittsburgh, the Pennsylvania Federation of Clubwomen, fifty thousand strong, protested. In Boston, the Massachusetts Federation of Churches shot off a hellfire-and-brimstone statement that would have warmed Cotton

Mather's heart. The Reverend Dr. Russell H. Conwell, president of Temple University, joined in the hurrahing. So did Rabbi Joseph Krauskopf of Temple Keneseth Israel in New York City, just to show that the spirit of brotherhood still lived. The Women's Christian Temperance Union somehow managed to get into the act.

The editors even gave space to the president of the Hathaway Shakespeare Club, curiously. That good lady, Mrs. Charles Irving Purnell by name, was not one to mince words or let herself get confused by the Golden Rule. She laid it right on the line, saying, "We must stop letting down the bars in matters like this. If society allows itself to be guided entirely by the Gospel rule, 'Let him who is without sin cast the first stone,' no one would ever be convicted for a crime. I do not believe in such ready forgiveness. Arbuckle is not the proper person to appear before the public. He has misbehaved and deserves punishment at the hands of the public."

He got it.

In California, a few weeks after his acquittal, Arbuckle looked at a fancy scrolled checkbook sent to him as a present by one of his few well-wishers outside Hollywood.

"I don't see why I should be sent a checkbook," he said sadly. "I haven't money enough now to make out one check, much less make use of a whole book."

For eleven long years, Arbuckle paid the penalty. They were years that looked like a montage out of a grade-B movie about show business—the old tearjerker about the veteran entertainer who keeps going downhill steadily, from one rough incident to another.

Arbuckle took a trip around the world, paid for by his Hollywood friends in the hope that the hue and cry would have died down by the time he got back; it didn't. He tried vaudeville and flopped; he just wasn't funny anymore. There was melancholy even in his laughter; his jokes, no matter what the subject, sounded somehow bitter. He appeared tired, and he was—tired of living a death-in-life. He wanted desperately to live again, a free man, as he once had lived, but that was denied him. He began an act at a Culver City nightclub and Prohibition agents promptly raided the joint.

Buster Keaton got him a job directing a comedy under the pseudonym of William Goodrich, his mother's maiden name. (The wags said he should have taken the name Will B. Good, and today there are some people who still think he did take that name, so powerful is legend.) But Arbuckle couldn't direct comedy anymore; he was short-tempered, grouchy, lacked patience, couldn't handle people. After he'd been working on the comedy a few days, William Randolph Hearst asked him to drop it and direct Hearst's "protégé," Marion Davies, in a film of Victor Herbert's musical, *The Red Mill.* Arbuckle accepted, not knowing that Buster Keaton had arranged the Hearst offer in order to ease Arbuckle off the comedy film. *The Red Mill* was a success of sorts, but it didn't give Arbuckle the comeback that he was always talking about.

He went on a road tour in a stage farce that flopped. He appeared in a revue in France, where his films had always had a big audience, and he was booed not because of l'Affaire Rappe but because his comedy act was so bad.

Despite the friends who remained loyal, Arbuckle's life was lonely after the scandal. He and his wife had been estranged at the time of his arrest, but she had rejoined him until his acquittal, affirming her faith in his innocence at every opportunity. Two years after the trial she divorced him. His second marriage, to Doris Deane, brought all his Hollywood friends out to celebrate. That marriage ended in divorce in 1929. In 1932 Arbuckle married for a third time. The bride was Addie Oakley Dukes McPhail, an actress who had been divorced from her first husband a week earlier. She was twenty-six, Roscoe forty-five. They were appearing in a vaudeville act in Cleveland at the time, and they motored to Erie, Pennsylvania, and woke up a justice of the peace at 2:30 in the morning to perform the ceremony.

Tall and lovely, Addie appeared to be what Arbuckle had always needed. She taught him gently to husband his strength, to eat sensibly, to save his money, to keep himself occupied. She never criticized him, and yet she managed to blunt the edge of the scarcely masked belligerence that was beginning to mark Arbuckle's manner.

Almost immediately after the wedding, the tide appeared to turn for Arbuckle. He got a contract from Warner Brothers to do a comedy short. He ambled into the old Vitaphone studio in Brooklyn, slipped into his old No. 12 shoes and the grey trousers that measured seventy-five inches around his fifty-inch waist, palmed his familiar brown derby, and mugged at the camera, a movie actor come home.

"It's a big thrill," he said.

He felt good. He'd managed to pay off more than two hundred thousand dollars in debts over the past eleven years from what he had earned and, although he was not yet in the clear, he owed less than five thousand. He felt that this marriage, at last, was right for him. He had the proud knowledge that he had not surrendered, that he had gone on fighting for his professional life against seemingly impossible odds, and now, although he was starting at the bottom again with two-reelers, he had at least won a place for himself again in the medium he loved. He felt confident that he could be as funny as ever. He had been blessed with what he considered a good omen: the first person he had seen after entering the studio was Joe Henaberry, a pal from the old Keystone Cops days and now a producer, who had directed Arbuckle's greatest success, *Brewster's Millions.*

Arbuckle thought he couldn't fail. For once, he was right. The first comedy pleased everybody at Warners and the studio contracted for some more comedy shorts. On June 28, 1933, he finished the last of the series at the studios in Astoria, Queens. During the last hour or two of work he stepped off the set and said to Ray McCarey, the director, "Do you mind if I knock off for a few minutes? I can't get my breath; I want a breath of fresh air." After a short respite, he finished the picture in high spirits.

The following night there was a party to celebrate the first anniversary of Addie and Roscoe's wedding. William La Hiff, a restaurant owner, was the host, and the party was a light-hearted affair, full of Broadway people who genuinely liked Arbuckle. To Joe Rivkin, his manager, Arbuckle said quietly during the party, "This is the happiest day of my life, Joe. It's a second honeymoon."

After the party began to break up, about midnight, Addie and Roscoe returned to their suite in the Park Central Hotel and retired for the night. About 3 a.m. Addie awoke and spoke to Roscoe. He didn't answer. She shook him. There was no reaction. Frightened and realizing what she refused to let herself think, she grabbed the telephone and called for the house doctor. A few minutes later the doctor took his stethoscope from the great chest of Roscoe Arbuckle and straightened up. "I'm sorry, Mrs. Arbuckle," the doctor said. "Your husband is dead."

The body lay in state in an undertaking establishment at

Sixty-sixth Street and Broadway, in the same room from which Rudolph Valentino, Jeanne Eagels, and June Matthews had been buried.

Two weeks later his widow reported to Surrogate's Court that Roscoe Arbuckle had left an estate of not more than two thousand dollars.

Twenty-five years later, the Hollywood Chamber of Commerce said that his name would be imbedded in a "Walk of Fame" as part of the "Hollywood Improvement Program."

3 William Desmond Taylor:
Who Killed the Mystery Man?

The Arbuckle Affair was still at its height—the comedian was awaiting his third trial—when the murder of William Desmond Taylor confronted Hollywood with a new scandal.

On January 14, 1922, Will Hays agreed to become the czar of the motion picture industry, and on March 6 he met for the first time with the biggest men in Hollywood to organize the group that became known as the Motion Picture Producers and Distributors of America.

Almost exactly midway between those two dates occurred the murder of Taylor, a handsome, cultivated former actor who had become chief director for Famous Players-Lasky Studios (later called Paramount) at a salary of one hundred thousand dollars a year. The murder, officially unsolved to this day, made Arbuckle's trouble appear like juvenile delinquency.

The Taylor case had everything: switched identities, a runaway husband and business man, sex, narcotics, gangsters, a disappearing witness, and innumerable celebrities. Before the furor subsided, the backwash from the case

A photograph inscribed to one of the women in the case: "To Mary Miles Minter, whose sweetness and sincerity has won the loyal friendship of William D. Taylor." *Los Angeles Times Photo*

brought in the names of two of the top movie queens of the day, Mabel Normand and Mary Miles Minter.

Hollywood in its wildest moments would never have tried to sell a scenario as melodramatic and farfetched as that to the public. But when life surpassed art, as it often does, Hollywood wished that it had never happened.

These were the principal figures in the strange story:

William Desmond Taylor—Nobody in Hollywood really knew much about the tall, patrician actor from England. He had appeared in the early 1910s as an actor in the movies. For several years he had worked as both actor and director before abandoning acting altogether. He had enlisted in the Canadian Army in 1918 but saw no action in the war. When he returned to Hollywood after the armistice he became not only a leading director but also president of the Motion Picture Directors Association.

At forty-five, Taylor was in his prime. Suave, soft-spoken, erudite, urbane, he charmed men and women alike. He had a considerable library and his conversation displayed an easy familiarity with its contents. Women usually found more than his mind to admire, and this didn't displease him at all. In a period when Hollywood made no pretense to morals, Taylor was considered a lecher of impressive proportions.

He often told his friends that he had never married.

Mabel Normand—A comic genius, Mabel Normand has seldom, if ever, been equaled by other film comediennes in the forty years since Taylor's murder.

She was born in Boston on November 10, 1894. When she was fourteen, she moved with her family to Staten Island in New York harbor. The following year she was posing as a model for Charles Dana Gibson, James Montgomery Flagg, and other artists.

A photographer recommended her to a movie maker as "the prettiest girl in New York" when she was sixteen, and she was promptly hired as an actress. She worked for Vitagraph and Biograph.

It was then that she met Mack Sennett, who was also working for Biograph. Three years later, in California, Sennett began producing movies for the Keystone Film Company, and Mabel Normand, whom he had summoned from New York, starred in the first Keystone comedy, *Cohen at Coney Island*.

Mabel and Sennett, who was a dozen years older, fell in love almost from the moment they met, and for years their romance was one of the few stable relationships in the emotionally shaky world of the film. They were expected to marry, and in 1915 they set the date. But two weeks before the wedding, Mabel surprised Sennett in the bedroom of her best friend, another actress, and that ended everything.

Sennett lost not only a wife but an actress as well when Miss Normand walked out. She was better at improvisation than any of the others in the Keystone comedies, and they were all good. On the day the Sennett troupe arrived in Los Angeles by train, for example, they stepped right into the middle of a Shriners' parade.

Miss Normand promptly grabbed a doll from the station gift shop, cuddled it in her arms as though it were a baby, and barged into the parade. Stopping in front of a dignified-looking Shriner, as the Sennett camera ground away, she informed the world that he was the heartless father of her poor little child of shame. This caused a good deal of confusion and argument, compounded when the other Keystone actors, who had quickly donned police costumes, descended upon the parade to right the little lady's wrong. When the real cops moved in to break up the row the cameraman, hard at work in a car marked "Press," caught it all.

Even the Sennett trademark—the custard pie as a weapon—originated with Mabel Normand. In the middle of a scene she decided that it was flagging in interest. Spotting a pie that some stagehands were about to eat for lunch, she grabbed it and flung it into Ben Turpin's face. When one of Sennett's production assistants ran to the set to find out what the commotion was all about, Mabel demonstrated what had happened by picking up another pie and pushing it into his face. And all the time the cameras were grinding.

Mary Miles Minter—Hailed as a second Mary Pickford, Mary Miles Minter was a top ingenue in films, the epitome of innocent maidenhood.

But much of MMM, as her fans called her, was not what it appeared to be. She had been christened Juliet Reilly at birth. Her birthplace was Shreveport, Louisiana, and the date was April 1, 1892. But during her entire career, under the dominance of her mother, Mrs. Charlotte Shelby (who had divorced Mary's father and remarried), she managed to make everyone believe that she was ten years younger than her real age.

Mabel Normand had little occasion to clown for the press when they learned she was the last person to see Taylor alive. They made mincemeat of her when word got out of a drug angle.

Eddie Brandt's Saturday Matinee

Ingenue Mary Miles Minter at 18 (give or take 10 years). When she kissed Taylor at the funeral, he whispered, "I shall always love you, Mary."

Eddie Brandt's Saturday Matinee

Separating fact from fiction in the biography of any movie actor has always been a difficult task; sometimes, as with Mary, it is impossible. She probably began her theatrical career as a child, for Mrs. Shelby was every inch the domineering stage mother. By 1915 MMM was appearing in *Barbara Frietchie* looking, as always, girlish, demure, and wholly innocent.

These three, Mary Miles Minter, Mabel Normand, William Desmond Taylor, were all victims of the killer who struck so unexpectedly that night in 1922.

Billy Taylor, as his friends called him, lived in a two-story, Spanish-style stucco cottage that was one of eight in a little court not far from Wilshire Boulevard, slightly east of Hollywood proper (or improper, as the case may be). His address was 404-B South Alvarado Street, which is now occupied by a business concern. Across Alvarado was Westlake Park, which the moviemakers of the day often used in their films.

Of all the houses in the court, Taylor's was undoubtedly the most interesting. At almost any hour of the day or night his neighbors, if they were nosy, and it turned out that they were, could see women arriving or departing; the interval between was rarely less than an hour.

A few actresses boasted of the invitations they had received and accepted to his house, but there were others who sounded bitter when they talked about it, who said that his "invitations" were more like commands. And nobody thought that the dashing Mr. Taylor, intellectual as he might be, wanted to play chess with his lovely guests.

On the night of February 1, at 6 o'clock, Taylor called Mabel Normand and told her he had two books for her; he asked her to pick them up. She immediately had her chauffeur drive her to Alvarado Street. She arrived there at 6:45 p.m. As Taylor's black butler, Henry Peavey, admitted her, Miss Normand could hear the director talking to someone on the telephone. Taylor sounded agitated. When Taylor realized that Mabel was waiting in the living room, he hung up and went in to greet her. He told Peavey to fix a cocktail for them and invited his guest to stay for dinner.

"No, darling, but thank you," she said. "I told Davis to keep the motor running because I'd be out in a jiffy. I'm tired and I want to go home."

Taylor said he was sorry. He produced the books, one about Sigmund Freud, the founder of psychoanalysis, the other an

X marks the spot where Taylor lived, in the Westlake district near Hollywood. Police found ladies' panties and compromising photographs there.

Part of the evidence was this photo of Mabel Normand inscribed "To my dearest." They found her love letters in his riding boots.

outline of German philosophy. "Sit down and I'll tell you about them," he suggested.

Peavey came in as the two sat on the couch talking about the books. The butler looked with dismay at the rug, where Miss Normand had been dropping peanut shells as she cracked them open for the nuts inside. He asked if Taylor wanted him to remain.

"You may go home, Henry," said Taylor.

Peavey left.

There was a pile of checks on Taylor's desk in the room. He had been working on his income-tax return. (In those halcyon days the tax on an income like his was a mere four percent.) That year Taylor had a special problem in computing his taxes, for in the year just past his valet, Edward F. Sands, had taken advantage of Taylor's absence in Europe to use his employer's charge accounts, pawn his jewelry, wreck two of his cars, and steal most of his clothes, vanishing just before Taylor returned. But even after Taylor's return, checks forged with Taylor's signature had been cashed at a great rate, and there had been two burglaries of the cottage as 1921 ended— all apparently the work of Sands.

"Look what that damned fellow Sands did to me," Taylor exclaimed to Miss Normand, pointing to the stack of checks. "Nearly every one of those checks is a forgery, and he did such a good job that to save my life I can't tell which are my signatures and which are his. I've been going over them about twenty times and I'm going mad!"

"Well, what are you going to do about it?" Miss Normand asked.

"If they ever find Sands, I'll do plenty," Taylor promised.

It had been about 7:15 p.m. when Peavey, who slept out, left the house. It was nearly 7:45 p.m. when Taylor walked Miss Normand to her car. The chauffeur, William Davis, held the door open for her. Taylor handed her the two books through the window. Then, Miss Normand was driven off in her car and Taylor went back into his cottage.

Both were unaware that one of Taylor's neighbors, Faith Cole McLean, first wife of actor Douglas McLean, had been an interested spectator of the leave-taking.

At 8:15 p.m., or thereabouts, Mrs. McLean's husband and two other residents of the court heard a sound that they decided later (the next day, in fact) must have been a shot. It couldn't have impressed them much at the time, for none of

Edna Purviance, Taylor's neighbor, slipped away to make two phone calls when police discovered bullets in Taylor's body. Edna was one of Chaplin's leading ladies, onstage and off.

The Museum of Modern Art/Film Stills Archive

the three looked out. However, a few minutes later, Mrs. McLean did happen to look out her window. She saw a man leave the Taylor house through the alley next to the director's garage.

Shortly after 8:15 p.m., in fact, a man did go to Taylor's house. He was Taylor's chauffeur, Howard Fellows. In accordance with earlier instructions from Taylor, he had telephoned the director's house several times, getting no answer. So he went to the house and rang the doorbell. Still no answer. He then put the car away and went home.

Later in the evening Edna Purviance, the famous star who was Charlie Chaplin's leading lady at the time, saw lights on in Taylor's house; Miss Purviance lived in the court, too. She ran across to his cottage to visit him. She rang the doorbell, but got no answer. Puzzled, she went home, probably assuming that Billy Taylor was entertaining a feminine guest.

The stage was now set for Hollywood's most spectacular murder case and one of its most earthshaking scandals.

It was Peavey who discovered the body.

The butler arrived at the house at 7:30 in the morning, as was his wont. He picked up the milk, opened the back door with his key, and walked into the kitchen. It was not until he walked into the living room that he saw the body that had been Billy Taylor twelve hours earlier. The dead man looked untroubled; his jacket was buttoned; his arms were at his side in relaxed fashion, his feet were together. He lay on his back near his desk.

"Mr. Taylor's dead! Mr. Taylor's dead!" Peavey shrieked as he ran out of the house into the court.

Doors and windows were thrown open hurriedly. Men and women appeared from all sides. There were excited voices. A crowd began to gather.

McLean had been one of the first to respond to Peavey's frantic cries. The actor stopped a doctor who happened to be passing the court. The physician went into the Taylor house, listened for a heartbeat, pronounced the director dead.

"He died of a gastric hemorrhage," the doctor said, pointing to a small brown stain scarcely noticeable in the corner of Taylor's mouth. It was dried blood. The doctor called the coroner and left.

In the meantime people had been arriving at Taylor's cottage: E. C. Jessurum, who owned the houses in the court; Charles Eyton, general manager of Famous Players-Lasky, and thus Taylor's boss; Harry Fellowes, Taylor's assistant director.

McLean, at the request of Eyton, carried Taylor's ample supply of illegal liquor away in order to spare his reputation, which was going to be hit by much nastier accusations, although Eyton didn't know it at the time. Fellowes, however, might have suspected what was to come, for he darted into the master bedroom in the confusion and collected letters and other memorabilia of past love affairs which might give some suspicious people ideas about Billy Taylor's morals.

As they stood about the body, several persons commented on how neatly the dead man lay there. As Eyton put it, "He looks almost as if he'd been laid out."

The assistant coroner, who had just arrived, nodded in agreement. The same thought had occurred to him. It suggested another, more sinister possibility to both him and Eyton.

"Turn him over!" Eyton cried. "Turn him over!"

The body was rolled over on its side. There was a dry brown stain on the carpet and there were two bullet holes in Billy Taylor's back. At that moment, for the first time, it was clear that the police were confronted with a case of murder.

Wild excitement flared through the crowd as the hushed word "Murder!" swept out from the house. Edna Purviance, who was in the house when the bullet wounds were discovered, stood still in horrified silence, but only for a moment. Then she slipped away to make two telephone calls.

The first call was to Mabel Normand. She nearly collapsed at the news. A few minutes later, however, several policemen arrived to question her, accompanied by reporters who had already heard that she was the last person known to have seen Taylor alive. It was probably good for Miss Normand's state of mind that they did arrive; they forced her to think about more than her grief and horror.

The other call was to Mary Miles Minter, who was then thirty years old, pretended to be twenty, and looked fifteen. Edna Purviance knew that MMM had been in love with Taylor; everybody knew it. Mary wasn't home when Miss Purviance called but her mother was, and she took the message.

Mary and her sister, Margaret, had been staying with Mrs. Shelby's mother, Mrs. Julia Branch Miles. Mrs. Shelby sped to Mrs. Miles' Hobart Street house to acquaint her daughter with the news. But Mary saw her mother coming and locked herself in her room, so she didn't hear Mrs. Shelby's excited cry, "Children! Mr. Taylor has been murdered!"

Mrs. Shelby kept pounding on the door to Mary's room. "Open this door!" she demanded. "I have something to tell you!"

Finally her daughter opened the door.

"Mr. Taylor was found murdered in his bed this morning!" Mrs. Shelby told her, not altogether accurately (although anyone might be pardoned for assuming that such a connoisseur of women would meet his fate at the scene of his favorite activities).

"Where were you last night?" Mrs. Shelby suddenly asked Mary.

Mary didn't answer the question. Her face went white. She looked as though she were about to faint. Then she suddenly seemed to catch hold of herself. She began hunting wildly for her car keys.

And all the while her mother kept shrieking at her. "You stay in this room and don't you dare leave until I tell you to," Mrs. Shelby shouted.

"Get away from that door!" Mary screamed back.

Mrs. Miles had the car waiting downstairs. She rode with her granddaughter to the bungalow court on Alvarado Street, but the police wouldn't let Mary into Taylor's house, despite an hysterical outburst by the young actress outside.

Then Mary Miles Minter drove to Mabel Normand's home for a woman-to-woman talk.

It would be interesting to know what those two women said to each other, for both had been understood to be engaged to Taylor. One was a great star and comic genius whom the director had found fascinating; the other was a top star and ingenue, off screen as well as on, who had found the director fascinating.

Each had a career at stake that day and both of them, even burdened with grief, knew it. Neither was taking any chances. After Mary arrived, Mabel took her into the bathroom for their private conversation "just in case there are any listening devices stuck around here," said Mabel, although "bugging" machines were uncommon then.

Nobody will ever know for sure just what was said in that room.

Back at Taylor's house, the police were searching for clues. They found that the bullet holes in Taylor's suit coat did not line up with the holes in his vest. They theorized that he had been seated at his desk, bent over writing, with his jacket higher than it would normally hang, when he was shot from behind.

Outside the back door was a pile of cigarette butts, proof that somebody had stood there, chain-smoking, apparently while Mabel Normand was visiting Taylor. It could have been the killer.

There was ample evidence of Billy Taylor's love affairs. In the living room were framed photographs of Miss Normand and Miss Minter, both ardently inscribed.

There was a scented note on stationery monogrammed "MMM." The note wasn't long, but it made its point. It read:

> "Dearest—
> "I love . . . I love you . . . I love you . . .
> "X X X X X X X X X X X X X X X X!
> > > > "Yours always,
> > > > "Mary"

They also found a handkerchief bearing Mary's monogram.

There were other items of interest in Taylor's house, including women's panties and sheer nightgowns. There were letters, too, dozens of love letters from many different women.

Some of the letters were in a code which was soon deciphered. One of the cipher letters went like this:

> "What shall I call you, you wonderful man? You are outstanding on the lot, the idol of an adoring company. You have just come over and put your coat on my chair. I want to go away with you, up in the hills or anywhere, just so we'd be alone—all alone. In a beautiful woodland lodge you'd be the cook (as I can only make tea) and fetch the water and build the fire. Wouldn't it be glorious to sit in a big, comfy couch by a cozy, warm fire with the wind whistling outside, trying to harmonize with the faint strains of music coming from the Victrola . . . and then you'd have to take off the record.
>
> "Of course I don't mean that, dear. Do you really suppose I intended you to take care of me like a baby? Oh, no, for this is my part: I'd sweep and dust (they make the sweetest little dust caps, you know) and tie fresh

ribbons on the snowy white curtains and feed the birds and fix the flowers and—oh, yes—set the table and help you wash the dishes and then in my spare time darn your socks.

"I'd go to my room and put on something scant and flowing; then I'd lie on the couch and wait for you. I might fall asleep, for a fire makes me drowsy. Then I'd wake to find two strong arms around me and two dear lips pressed on mine in a long, sweet kiss . . ."

The young woman who wrote the letter was obviously of an ardent nature.

Another cipher letter, decoded, read:

"I love you—oh, I love you so! I had to come down because Mamma remarked that I always seemed to feel rather happy after being out with you. So here I am. Camouflage.

"Furthermore, I am feeling unusually fine. (More camouflage.) I will see you later. God love you, as I do."

There were other clues, including a handkerchief initialed "S" which was near Taylor's body when he was found and three blonde hairs found beneath the collar of the coat the director was wearing when he was slain.

Robbery was definitely not the motive. When his body was found, Taylor was still wearing his two-carat diamond ring and his platinum wristwatch and in his pockets the police found seventy-eight dollars.

But what was the motive?

Detectives got wind of a row between Mable Normand and Billy Taylor and questioned her about it. The argument had occurred a month earlier, on New Year's Eve.

At that time the two were understood to be engaged. Taylor took Miss Normand to a party at the Alexandria Hotel, then a favorite night spot. But he became angry with her because he thought she drank too much and flirted with many of the men.

"I said to him, 'For God's sake, why do you stand around with that trick dignity of yours? You make me sick!' or something like that," Miss Normand told the police.

"And he said, 'I'm not trying to be dignified. Good God, don't you know I like you?' And I said, 'Good God, don't be so melodramatic!' and then I guess I sulked and wouldn't talk and he left me with a hurt expression."

A few days later it was learned that the dead man's house had been ransacked a day or two after the murder. To this day nobody really knows what the intruder was searching for, but his—or her—object may have been other letters.

Mabel Normand, for example, had written eight or nine love letters to Taylor; after his death she sought them in a drawer of his desk, where she knew he always kept them. They weren't there.

At this point Miss Normand, on the verge of a nervous breakdown, admitted hysterically that she had gone to Taylor's house on the night of the murder, not to borrow the books, but to get her letters back. When she arrived at his house, she said, Taylor told her that he had mailed the letters to her the day before.

"I replied that they had not yet arrived," Miss Normand said, "and then he said, 'I think either Eyton or Garbutt has them.'"

A week after the murder, while Eyton and some detectives were in Taylor's house, the letters were found in the toe of one of his boots in the closet of his bedroom, having obviously been placed there after the discovery of the crime.

It was never established who put them there.

The greatest sensation in the case came a few days later.

The public, which had been avidly reading everything that was printed about the Taylor murder, and Hollywood, which had been worried by the possible consequences of the case, were equally startled to learn that William Desmond Taylor had been engaged in an elaborate masquerade.

He was not at all the man they had thought him to be.

His real name, they learned, was William Cunningham Deane-Tanner, nicknamed "Pete" in his youth. He was born in Ireland, in County Cork, in 1877, the son of a British army officer. Pete's father was one of three brothers, two of whom died under mysterious circumstances in Ireland. Pete's grandfather, a physician in Cork, also met a violent end; his mangled body was found near a railroad track, and the circumstances of his death remained unexplained.

His father had wanted Pete to become an army officer, too, but the boy's eyesight was not up to army standards. Pete went to Clifton College at Bristol, registering under the Taylor pseudonym—why, no one knows. He left Clifton in 1895 and went into show business as secretary to a theatrical troupe then playing in Manchester. His father, disappointed and angered, sent him to work on a ranch in Kansas. From there the youth made his way to New York, where Pete and his brother, Denis, operated a Manhattan art and antiques shop (Taylor was then using his real name, Deane-Tanner). Pete married one of the original Floradora Girls who bore him a daughter. They lived in the fashionable suburb of Larchmont.

Mrs. Deane-Tanner's uncle was Daniel J. Braker, a multi-millionaire realtor and importer. Pete borrowed a great deal of money from Braker but confided to his friends that his extravagances were all right because he expected to be taken care of handsomely in Braker's will. In June 1907, however, Braker married Mrs. William H. Gelshenen, who was called "the ten-million-dollar widow" when Braker died a year later.

In October 1908, Braker's will was filed for probate. One of its clauses read:

"To W.C.D. Tanner, I leave and bequeath the amounts of money owing to me by him."

Pete's hopes of a big legacy were completely destroyed. Financial and personal disaster faced him, unless he could think of a way out of his difficulties.

On October 23, 1908, Pete left his home and went to the city, where he began to drink heavily. He didn't go to the shop or back to his home that night.

On the next day, October 24, he attended the Vanderbilt Cup race on Long Island with some friends.

On October 26 he sent a note to his assistant at the art shop, asking that six hundred dollars be sent to him at the Broadway Central Hotel. The assistant found Deane-Tanner there, weary and haggard, and with his mustache shaved off. Pete pocketed one hundred dollars and mailed five hundred to his wife. Then he vanished. His family never saw him again.

His brother Denis, who had always depended on him, lost the shop and went to work managing another art shop on East Forty-fifth Street.

A month after Pete's disappearance, Denis' wife presented him with a daughter. Two years later a second child was born. At that time the Denis Deane-Tanners lived at 247 West One Hundred and Fourth Street.

In 1912 Pete's wife obtained a New York divorce, not for desertion, which was and is not grounds for divorce in New

York State, but for adultery. Under the name of "Townsend," Mrs. Deane-Tanner said, her husband had spent a week at an Adirondacks hotel with a beautiful girl some time before his disappearance.

In the same year, 1912, Denis' wife developed tuberculosis and was sent to the Adirondacks for treatment. While she was in the sanitorium, Denis followed his brother's example. Denis vanished, too.

Two years later, in 1914, some friends of Mrs. W.C. Deane-Tanner went to see a movie in the Hamilton Theater in Yonkers. They were astonished to see that the male lead was Pete Deane-Tanner himself, although he was listed in the credits as William Desmond Taylor (he had kept the same initials, as most men using false names do).

There was a second surprise in the film: the blacksmith was played by Pete's brother Denis!

The friends quickly told Pete's ex-wife, who wrote to Taylor in care of the studio. He began a regular correspondence with her and their daughter. Later that year his ex-wife married the owner of Delmonico's Restaurant.

None of this, of course, had been known to Billy Taylor's friends in Hollywood.

With this new information about Taylor's background, some things began to make sense to the police, at least in theory. For example, Sands, Taylor's larcenous valet, had pawned the goods he had stolen from Taylor. Sands gave the pawn-broker the name of William Cunningham Deane-Tanner, Taylor's real name, which was unknown to Hollywood. Moreover, Sands had mailed the pawn tickets to Denis' wife, who was living at Monrovia, near Pasadena, on a fifty-dollar-a-month pension from Taylor.

Was Sands really Denis Deane-Tanner?

To this day no one knows.

But even allowing for the knowledge that a valet may gain about his master, Sands seems to have been far too familiar with Billy Taylor's background to have been merely a man-servant. But if he were Denis, why did he pillage his brother's house and bank account in his absence?

Again we come to a stone wall: no one knows.

Sands, who had disappeared before Taylor returned from Europe, has never been found. The police searched all over the world for him for more than a quarter of a century, even exhuming a body from a Hartford, Connecticut grave because they thought it might be he. It wasn't.

If Sands were alive today he'd be about ninety-five. Is he alive? Or could he have been murdered, too? The questions are innumerable. There are no answers.

The theories about Taylor's death opened a tremendous range of suspects. Narcotics opened a whole world of speculation, for example.

A few weeks before his death Taylor had gone to the federal narcotics agents of his own volition to tell them what he knew about the dope traffic in Hollywood. In our time there is a thriving traffic in narcotics in Hollywood, but in Taylor's time narcotics addiction was almost epidemic.

Taylor didn't use drugs, but Mabel Normand was an addict, and it was apparently his bitterness about her addiction that led him to the federal men.

Had the director become a menace to the freedom and peace of mind of the gangsters behind the narcotics ring?

Narcotics, sex, and blackmail were all tied together in many ways. Taylor had been deeply involved in the hectic sex life of Hollywood. Police were already aware that a good many blackmailers, preying on the stars' weaknesses for sex and drugs, were busily at work mining the gold in the Hollywood hills.

Had Taylor threatened to turn the tables on a blackmailer and expose him? Or had someone suspected, because of the variety of Taylor's sex life, that the director was feeding information to blackmailers?

The gangsters—this was in the Roaring Twenties, when the mobs rode high—had been moving in on Hollywood. There was a rumor that Taylor had had a falling-out with a bootlegger who supplied a large part of the liquor consumed in Hollywood.

Was the Taylor murder a gang rubout?

Then there were other problems to consider. Mabel Normand had quarreled bitterly with Taylor a month earlier. Mrs. Shelby had a .38 caliber pistol just like the one that shot Taylor. Mary Miles Minter had been staying out very late at night for some time before the murder. Peavey, Taylor's butler, had been arrested on a morals charge in a park a short time before the murder, although he protested his innocence in his high, falsetto voice.

Who killed William Desmond Taylor, the last of a blood-stained Irish line? A castoff woman? A jealous man? His brother (Sands?)? A blackmailer? A narcotics racketeer? A bootlegger?

The suspects, like the possible motives, were legion. Nobody ever was able to single out one suspect and one motive and say, "This is why Billy Taylor died, and this is his murderer."

Unlike movie killers, who must always meet their doom in the end, Billy Taylor's murderer escaped, undetected to this day.

In the end, careers were ruined and reputations destroyed, and all for naught.

Mabel Normand emerged from the scandal with only a precarious hold on her career. The public, linking her with all the vice that was being exposed in Hollywood, took a rather dim view of her for a time, but she was not driven into complete exile as Fatty Arbuckle was.

But bad luck still pursued her, undoubtedly because her judgment had not improved. Late in December 1923, her physician ordered Mabel into a hospital for an appendectomy.

"Whoever heard of appendicitis on New Year's Eve?" she snorted. "Not I. Tonight I'll see the old year out. They can have my appendix tomorrow."

She went from the doctor's office to the home of Edna Purviance, arriving early for a New Year's Eve party. Later that night Courtland S. Dines, a Denver oil millionaire, caught a bullet from a gun fired by Mabel's chauffeur, Horace A. Greer, whom she had hired after the Taylor murder. Dines recovered and Greer was released by police, but the full fury of public indignation fell upon Mabel Normand this time. The general belief was that the shooting had been the result of an argument over her favors. As Gene Fowler later wrote, "A lady is fortunate, indeed, if she can explain one scandal. The woman never lived who was resourceful enough to explain two."

Her career was over. Even her being named co-respondent in a divorce suit a year later couldn't make her troubles any worse.

Still in love with her, Mack Sennett starred her in two films, *Susanna* and *The Extra Girl.* Both were boycotted all over the country.

"It's no use," she said. "I'm a liability to everyone."

Financially secure—she had invested her money carefully, most of it in real estate that kept appreciating in value—Mabel went into an enforced retirement. She continued to live as part of the film colony, however.

Mary Miles Minter and her mother Charlotte Selby met outside the courtroom when the case reopened 15 years later. Both women were suspects but the case was never officially solved. *Evening News*

In 1926 she attempted a screen comeback in a Hal Roach film, *Raggedy Ann*. But the public had neither forgotten nor forgiven, as though Miss Normand had done anything requiring the forgiveness of the fickle public! Moviegoers remained away from her picture, which proved to be a devastating box-office flop.

After a party in her home one night, she went with Lew Cody, an old friend and co-worker of many years, woke up a license clerk and a minister in Ventura, and married Cody, one of the Keystone comedy stars. That was September 19, 1926. It was an unusual marriage, to say the least; they maintained her house and his, lived first at one, and then at the other.

On February 22, 1930, she died in her sleep in a hospital at Monrovia, after more than a year of fighting the slow advance of tuberculosis.

Toward the end of the following year, Peavey, Taylor's butler, died of general paresis in a mental hospital at Napa.

The only major figures in the case who remained alive were Mary Miles Minter and her mother, Mrs. Shelby. For Mary, the Taylor murder had proved disastrous, too.

It had been rather romantic at first. When she kissed her dead lover's lips before the funeral, she told reporters that she had been rewarded with a whisper from that lifeless mouth, "I shall love you always, Mary." The tabloids played up her ghoulish yarn for all it was worth.

In a short time, however, it became apparent that MMM was through in motion pictures, despite the efforts of some leaders of the industry to save her career (and their investment in her pictures). As the widely publicized, sweet, young innocent, she had the most to lose in a scandal. Her public image, as a later generation would put it, had been destroyed. The public wasn't in a mood for her films.

Moreover, scandal was piled on scandal for Mary as the investigation progressed. One of the more fantastic incidents that came to light involved the celebrated actor, James Kirkwood, who had been one of Mary's first directors.

When Mary was believed by her public and her movie associates to be fifteen, she and Kirkwood went wandering hand in hand through the countryside near Santa Barbara. Carried aways by their grand passion, they decided to "marry" each other on the spot without benefit of clergy.

So Kirkwood lifted Mary up on a rock, knelt at her feet, and said, "I, James, take you, Mary, for my wife in the sight of God."

This bit would be too corny for a modern teenager, but those were less sophisticated times. The whole thing went over big with Mary; too big, according to later testimony by her sister Margaret.

Little Mary fell for the mock ceremony so completely, according to her sister's sworn testimony, that she later became pregnant. The unfortunate aftermath was an abortion, Margaret revealed.

Kirkwood refused to discuss the matter because "it

wouldn't be gallant." What he didn't say was that he was already legally endowed with a wife at the time of the incident. She was Gertrude Robinson, his first wife. Later he married—in the eyes of the law as well as God—Lila Lee and, still later, Beatrice Powers. He never married Mary Miles Minter legally.

The scandals also brought to light the life that Mary had led under her mother's domination. Norman Sterry, an attorney who opposed both Mrs. Shelby and Mary in one court fight, said: "Up to the time she became of age, Mary turned over all her earnings to Mrs. Shelby. After she became of age, her mother signed a contract with her through which she was to receive thirty percent of her earnings.

"The fact is that Mary was allowed nothing, while her sister, Margaret, had everything. Mary was violently unhappy during those years, for her mother and sister were accusing her of intimacies with men and keeping her indebted to them at all times."

Mary Miles Minter earned more than a million and a half during her movie career. In 1924 she and her mother set up a trust fund which was terminated by court order at their request in 1956. At that time the account was said to amount to one hundred thousand dollars.

For a time after the murder, Mary and her mother were estranged. Everybody in Hollywood had known that Mrs. Shelby had been doing everything possible to end the romance between the daughter and the dashing director. But it was not until two years after the slaying, when Mary unburdened herself publicly, that a reason for her mother's attitude was exposed.

"Mother's actions over Mr. Taylor's attention to me," Mary said, "were not inspired by a desire to protect me from him. She was really trying to shove me into the background so that she could try to monopolize his attentions and, if possible, his love.

"He used to call at our house. But as soon as mother saw his preference for me, she put a stop to his visits . . . She cared for him herself."

In the years that followed, the focus of the investigation swung about from one person to another, from this place to that. Within six weeks of the murder, three hundred men and women had confessed to it, including some in Europe. A Tucson accountant was detained as a hot suspect; he was later released, cleared by any connection with the crime. As late as 1937 newspapers were still carrying headlines that the case had been broken, but the papers were skeptical. A typical headline said: "Taylor Murder Is Solved Again."

But back to Mrs. Shelby and her daughters came the investigators, again and again.

Mrs. Shelby was accused by a witness of having gone to Taylor's house and threatened him. She denied it.

Police found .38 caliber bullets in the foundation of a house Mrs. Shelby had lived in on New Hampshire Street. She said she knew nothing about them.

A broker who embezzled some of her money told Mrs. Shelby that he'd have her indicted for the Taylor murder if she complained about him. She had him sent to prison for the embezzlement. She was not indicted.

Mrs. Shelby and Margaret had a row, and Margaret, her favorite daughter, went off to the police with a new story. She said her mother had tossed "the gun" into the river at Kansas City on her way to New York by train. Mrs. Shelby promptly had Margaret committed to the psychopathic ward of the Los Angeles County Hospital, saying she'd been an alcoholic for three years and didn't know what she was talking about. A grand jury looked into the whole mess but returned no indictment.

About the same time, the district attorney announced officially that Mary Miles Minter had never been under suspicion for the crime. He did not say anything about her mother.

Mary never married. Under the name of Juliet Shelby she became a successful interior decorator in Los Angeles. She took care of her mother, who lived well into her eighties.

As far as the district attorney's office is concerned, the file on the murder of William Desmond Taylor is still open.

4 Paul Bern:

Why Did Jean Harlow's Husband Die?

For a decade after the scandals that brought the Hays
Office into being there was relative tranquillity, on the surface,
in Hollywood. There were several reasons for this. One was
that the stars were behaving with slightly more circumspec-
tion now, the example of Arbuckle, Minter, Normand, La Marr,
and many others still fresh in their minds. Many of those fallen
stars were still around Hollywood in those days. Another
reason was the organized power and unity of the motion
picture industry. Politicians who were unwilling to grant
special favors to the industry were ruthlessly fought. Police
chiefs were brought under the heel of the studio bosses. The
Hollywood correspondents were systematically prostituted;
those who insisted on covering all the news, the unfavorable
as well as the favorable, were barred from access to the stars
and the other studio personnel. Without entrée to the sources
of news, these honest correspondents were scooped every
day; they lost their usefulness to their newspapers. In time,
they were replaced with reporters who were more willing to
close their eyes to the seamy side of Hollywood. A few honest

reporters stuck it out, of course, but they were a lonely lot.

Of course, there were a few flurries in spite of everything, but they didn't amount to much. Chicago mobster Spike O'Donnell tried to get Hollywood to let him become an actor—he wanted to play Robin Hood—but the studios turned him down, despite his obvious merits as an expert on the subject. Clara Bow, the "It" girl, attracted a good deal of attention with her scorching love affairs with Gary Cooper, Harry Richman, Gilbert Roland, director Victor Fleming, and innumerable football players, cops, and other odd and assorted varieties of men. Miss Bow's reputation was damaged beyond repair in 1930 when her ex-secretary, Daisy De Voe, during a court battle with Clara, testified that the "It" girl used up her huge income on one parasitic boyfriend after another. Paramount dropped her the next year.

By that time, the "It" girl had already lost her place as the foremost sex queen of Hollywood to a newcomer, Jean Harlow. Before two years of her reign had expired, Miss Harlow would be involved in the biggest scandal in a decade; a scandal involving the mysterious death of her bridegroom, the suicide of his former mistress, and the threat of a criminal indictment against the star herself.

Jean Harlow was a platinum blonde (she dyed her hair but didn't admit it even to her press agent) who looked brassy, sounded brassy, and played brassy parts. And there were those in Hollywood who swore that her heart was solid brass, too. But then, there are always people who'll say things like that in Hollywood.

Her real name was Harlean Carpentier. She was born in Kansas City on March 3, 1911. She was destined to have a short life; whether it was merry only she could have said, but an objective observer would tend to doubt that there was much merriment in it, except on the surface. Harlean Carpentier was a fey creature, and she always seemed to sense her fate.

Before she was sixteen her parents separated. Her mother lived in Highland Park, a suburb of Chicago. It was there that young Harlean met Charles F. McGrew II, playboy son of a rich Chicago family. She was sixteen, he twenty-one, when they ran off to nearby Waukegan and were married on September 21, 1927. The young couple went to Beverly Hills to live, probably because Harlean wanted to break into the movies.

Harlow, Hollywood's first platinum blonde, had to don a red wig for M.G.M.'s *Red-Headed Woman*. Stepfather Marino Bello was determined to control her career—and her check book.

The Museum of Modern Art/Film Stills Archive

Under the name Jean Harlow she got extra work in several films, including one in which Clara Bow starred.

McGrew objected to his young wife's attempts to break into the movies, but she paid little attention to his protests. Finally she sued for divorce: McGrew, back in Chicago by then, decided to fight the divorce action. In his reply to her complaint, he told the court that Jean had posed for indecent pictures. She, in ·turn, conceded that she had posed au naturel, but she insisted that she had bared her charms only for "art photographs" taken by a reputable photographer. In the end, Jean and her husband agreed to a quiet divorce. He agreed to give her their house in Beverly Hills, an automobile, and an allowance of $375 a month—not bad money in those Depression days.

Just how Jean Harlow got her big break in films is still unclear. But it was Howard Hughes who discovered her, and Hughes' quaint and less than Victorian attitude toward women has long been a Hollywood legend, off-screen as well as on. Petite (five foot three) and trim (one-hundred-and-twelve pounds), the blue-eyed blonde with the dark eyebrows was just the sort of girl who'd interest Hughes. As an actress.

Hughes had a picture, *Hell's Angels,* which had been completed as a silent movie with Greta Nissen as the star. Then the talkies became the rage overnight. Nobody wanted to see a silent movie anymore. *Hell's Angels* had to be remade with dialogue. Jean Harlow got the feminine lead.

With the role—the picture was about fliers in the First World War—Jean also began her big publicity buildup. The first publicity picture of her in a Los Angeles newspaper carried the caption: "Sexquisite." Besides her platinum blonde hair, she became notable for her dresses, which were cut very low in front. This seemed a little pointless, for she was not particularly buxom, at least not by present-day standards.

Hell's Angels made Jean Harlow an immediate sensation. It was obvious that the process, not altogether deliberate, that produces a Nita Naldi, a Clara Bow, a Rita Hayworth, a Kim Novak, a Marilyn Monroe was at work. In later days, Jean would have been called a "sex bomb," as Miss Hayworth, Miss Novak, and Miss Monroe one day were to be. Miss Harlow was the rage of Hollywood. She was the hottest copy of the press corps.

The columns were filled with her dates, but observant readers might have noticed that she scarcely, if ever, went out with actors. Her escorts were always producers or directors. Perhaps Jean Harlow, a girl who knew how to take care of herself, had watched Norma Shearer and taken lessons from the career of that actress, who had married Irving Thalberg, production boss at Metro-Goldwyn-Mayer, and had promptly become the No. 1 actress on the lot.

It was a coincidence that Jean's next picture, *Red-Headed Woman,* was made for MGM. Thalberg's general assistant, Paul Bern, had persuaded Hughes to sell Jean's contract to MGM. Then Bern had fought to get the *Red-Headed Woman* lead for Miss Harlow. After that, he starred her in *Jungle Skies.* The leading role in the latter screenplay had been intended originally for Clara Bow. The circle had now come full tilt. Clara Bow's role had gone to a girl who once had been an extra in the "It" girl's pictures.

In the tradition of all the cliché-ridden films about Hollywood, a star had been born—thanks to Paul Bern.

It would be difficult to find two people more unalike than Jean Harlow and Paul Bern.

In the files of one New York newspaper today, the files on tens of thousands of persons are tabbed with an identifying phrase: "inventor," "painter," and so on. The envelope that contains the old, yellowed, crumbling clippings about this man is labeled: "Paul Bern—Genius."

That is how most of his contemporaries thought of Bern. Introspective, intellectual, sensitive, esthetic, humane, he would have been rare in any group of men. That such a man could find a niche for himself, and a very comfortable, profitable niche, at that, in Hollywood proves that the motion picture industry had a higher regard for intelligence than it was usually credited as possessing.

He was born Paul Levy, in Wannsbeck, Germany, on December 3, 1889, which made him twenty-two years older than Jean Harlow. His parents migrated to New York when he was nine. At fourteen his formal schooling ended, although those who met him later in life always assumed that he was highly educated. He was, but he was self-educated.

His first job was with the Produce Exchange Company; he earned $3.50 a week. Then he worked for the gas company while learning stenography in night school. After he got a job as a stenographer, he began to write. He entered the Academy of Dramatic Arts and devoted his entire time to the theater, first as an actor with a small traveling troupe, later as

Clara Bow married Rex Bell when Harlow took over as the new "It" girl. Paramount was taking no chances after details of Clara's sex life were sold to a tabloid.
The Museum of Modern Art/Film Stills Archive

a stage manager, and finally, in 1912, as director of a stock company.

After a brief stint as a press agent, he got into the motion picture business by going to work for the Canadian Picture Company in Toronto. He also changed his name to Paul Bern. He quickly realized that everything important in pictures was developing in Hollywood, so he headed west. After landing a job as a film cutter in Samuel Goldwyn's laboratory, he worked his way into the scenario department, became a script editor, directed some movies, and at thirty-seven, became a supervisor at MGM. It was not long before he became Thalberg's general assistant.

In a remarkably prophetic article, Herbert Knight Cruikshank, writing in the *Morning Telegraph* in 1927, said, "Meet Paul Bern, and know that you stand in the presence of one blessed or cursed with the fearsome, terrible quality that sears souls, destroys the minds it so brilliantly lights, that with the fiery fury of a flagellant whips its slaves on to accomplishment—to immortality—to death. I mean the tragic quality of genius."

A trifle flowery, perhaps, but unquestionably true of Paul Bern.

Cruikshank described Bern for his readers: "A slight man, insignificant in stature, slender of shoulder, only as tall as a girl. He has a deal of forehead, topped with a mop of hair, soft and finespun—beautiful, perhaps, in a woman, in a man quite probably presaging premature baldness . . . The eyes . . . are slightly bulging and deeply circled with a sooty rim that seems to make them smoulder and then flash fire much in the fashion of live coals lying in the smoky gray and burned-out black of ashes."

The brilliance of intellect was accompanied by a temperament far more compassionate than most. "Hollywood's Father Confessor," they called him. Everybody took his troubles to Paul Bern for advice, sympathy, and help. When Barbara La Marr, poverty-stricken, was dying from the results of her addiction, Bern bought her a house in Altadena, hired the best doctors and 'round-the-clock nurses, and was at her bedside himself when death came.

There was one peculiarity about Bern. He thought that every movie ought to have a happy ending. Perhaps his feeling was prompted by the same sensitivity to other people's sorrows that made him such a friend in need. Sad endings left the audience depressed.

He hated unhappy endings.

Bern took little part in Hollywood's social life. Indeed, he was considered something of a mystery man. He lived in such an out-of-the-way place that he had to put a sign on the highway, beside a little dirt road, saying: "This way to Bern's house." He spent a good part of his time secluded in his home, reading. Occasionally he appeared at the bigger, and more conventional, parties (never the wild ones) and from time to time he might be seen in a nightclub.

When he began appearing in public with Jean Harlow, nobody placed any significance in it. Everyone was startled, therefore, when the couple showed up at the Marriage License Bureau to obtain a wedding permit. "We were surprised ourselves," Miss Harlow said. "Mr. Bern did not make the proposal until Sunday, and I accepted. We had casually spoken of marriage before, but not until Sunday was the subject seriously gone into. It was then we decided to get a license." The next day Jean dashed into a fashionable dress shop and chose a ready-made white dress with a fringed shawl to be her wedding gown. The day after they gathered with one hundred and fifty friends in the home of Jean's mother, who was now married to Marino Bello. Among the guests were Irving Thalberg and his wife, Norma Shearer.

And there on July 2, 1932, they were married—the fey actress and the genius with death in his eyes.

Work commitments forced them to postpone their honeymoon for a few months. They took one day off from work, then returned to the studio.

In the weeks that followed, Jean looked radiant. She often told her friends, "Paul is so magnificently eager to make me happy, I will never do anything to make him unhappy."

Bern, enjoying a quiet drink with a couple of close friends, told them, "After we were married a week I realized how wonderful Jean is. I'm more in love with her than ever. If my life were ended tomorrow I would have no complaint. I could only say it was full and complete because of the happiness I've had with Jean as my wife."

But as the weeks wore on, others noticed that Paul Bern didn't look happy. He seemed distraught. He was pale, almost haggard. Thalberg and other friends tried to indicate tactfully that they'd be available to talk over things if anything were troubling Paul, but he never took them up on the offers. If something was festering in his mind, he kept it to himself.

Inevitably, speculation turned to Bern's marriage. It was rumored that the couple were quarrelling about money. One of the arguments, it was said, centered about the mansion that he had given her as a wedding present. The house was set in the midst of five acres of land in Benedict Canyon. In 1932, that year of Depression when deflation had sent the value of the dollars skyrocketing, the mansion had cost sixty thousand dollars; an equivalent estate today would cost perhaps a quarter of a million dollars. But Jean didn't like the great house. She wanted to sell it and buy another house closer to her mother.

For Jean was, as Bern had come to learn, very much a "mama's girl."

On September 1 Bern was examined by a physician for the Prudential Insurance Company. The physician approved him as a good risk. Bern had applied for an eighty-five-thousand-dollar life insurance policy.

Four days later on September 5, 1932, two months after his marriage, Paul Bern was found shot to death in the Benedict Canyon house.

The butler found the body. He went running for his wife who was the cook. Then he called MGM at once. The studio security officer in charge that day—it was Labor Day—immediately notified the head of security for the studio, W.P. (Whitey) Hendry, who was at home in Santa Monica. Hendry put in two fast phone calls to Louis B. Mayer, the head of MGM, and to Thalberg, and then sped to Benedict Canyon.

Mayer beat him there. Thalberg and Hendry were next on the scene. But it was not until two hours later that the police were notified of the death. What happened in those two hours will probably never be known.

When the police finally arrived, Mayer left. As he drove down the driveway, he spotted Howard Strickling, the publicity chief for the studio, who was just arriving. Strickling stopped and Mayer and he talked briefly.

"Paul left a note." Mayer told him. "I decided it shouldn't be seen by anyone outside the studio, Howard, so I took it. Here it is."

Strickling was aghast. "You can't do that," he told his boss.

Howard Hughes and Bette Davis at a 1938 "Tailwaggers" party. Hughes, who dated Harlow and Monroe, had a quick eye for a nice bosom and a pretty face.   *The Museum of Modern Art / Film Stills Archive*

Harlow and Bern the day of their wedding. Two months later Bern was dead. What "frightful wrong" did he want to wipe out?   *Los Angeles Times Photo*

"This is a homicide investigation. If anyone ever finds out you took that, there'll be a God-awful stink. You've got to go back and give it to the cops."

Mayer turned around and drove back to the house. He gave the note to the police.

The note read:

"Dearest dear:

"Unfortunately, this is the only way to make good the frightful wrong I have done you and to wipe out my abject humiliation. I love you.

Paul."

A postscript said:

"You understand that last night was only a comedy."

The police read the note, tried for a moment to figure out its meaning, and then went back to examining the body.

Bern apparently had been shot while standing, nude, before a full-length mirror in his dressing room. The bullet, a .38 caliber slug, had entered his right temple, torn through his brain, and emerged at the back of the head to bury itself in the wall. The body was lying face down, the head turned with the right cheek against the carpet. The death weapon, a revolver, lay six feet from the body. On the dresser in his bedroom was another pistol, a .38 caliber automatic.

Detective Joseph Whitehead, who took charge of the investigation, said it was obviously a "straight suicide." But Chief of Detectives Taylor said there were discrepancies in the suicide theory. He ordered a more intensive investigation. Among other things, he wanted to know the reason for the long delay in notifying the police.

As part of the investigating group began going over the house and grounds, others questioned the gardener and the chauffeur. Still more detectives were sent to the Bello home to question Miss Harlow. They were unable to do so for some time, however, because her physician had decided she was too hysterical to undergo the ordeal.

Reporters outside the Bello home heard the famous Harlow voice cry out again and again, "Isn't this too terrible! But I mustn't talk about it—I can't! I can't!"

Police said that the servants had all told them that Miss Harlow and her husband had gotten along very well together. (This would be disputed much later.)

Eventually Miss Harlow talked to the police. She was not called as a witness at the inquest, however, which was a very unusual omission. The questions asked of others who did testify at the coroner's inquiry were often less than searching.

The story that emerged, at that point, was this:

Bern had sent his wife over to stay with her mother, who was alone, on Saturday night. On Sunday she returned to Benedict Canyon to share a "pickup dinner" with Bern, and then he sent her back to the Bello home, telling her he'd be along later after he finished reading some scenarios. When he didn't show up she thought nothing of it, assuming that he hadn't been able to get his work done.

The motive for the "suicide"?

The official suggestion was that Bern had been suffering from a physical infirmity that would have made a normal married life impossible. Less discreet sources put a name on the infirmity: impotence.

The fact that a man suffering from such a condition would not be likely to marry any woman, least of all a woman like Jean Harlow, was ignored by officialdom.

And then came the disclosure that Paul Bern had lived, in an apparently normal way, with another woman for many years. And the day after Bern's body was found, that woman, too, died under mysterious circumstances.

Dorothy Millette was an exquisite blonde who was struggling to become an actress when Bern met her. They lived together as man and wife in New York and Toronto for many years. She always used the name of Mrs. Paul Bern.

Then she fell victim to mental illness. It was necessary for her to enter a hospital. Paul paid all her expenses and visited her regularly for years. The love affair died during that time, but his real fondness for her continued. For the rest of her life he supported her.

When Dorothy was able to leave the sanitarium, she moved into a room at the Algonquin Hotel in Manhattan. There she lived quietly, reading a great deal and winning the admiration and respect of everyone on the staff. Bern saw her whenever he was in New York; the feeling between them was obviously warm and deep. In a 1920 will he left his estate to her. (That will was superseded, at his death, by a later testament leaving everything to Jean Harlow.)

In March 1932, Bern wrote a letter to his onetime mistress

that showed, better than anything else, the relationship between them. In it he said:

"Dear Dorothy:

"I was very happy to get your letter of March 17.

"I have been desperately trying to get away from here for both a vacation and change of scene for the last year, but so far it has been quite impossible.

"I read with great interest that you are contemplating a trip to San Francisco. Of course, I cannot give you any advice because you yourself can be the only person to know what is best. If you do go I hope that it will be a happy change.

"I understand that the Plaza Hotel is a fairly reasonable and attractive one.

"If you do change to any other place we will find some way of supplying you with funds in a manner convenient for you.

"My love and best wishes always,

Paul

"P.S. The Clift Hotel is, I believe, quite fashionable and not very expensive."

In May Bern's secretary sent a letter to Dorothy at the Plaza Hotel in San Francisco. It said:

"Dear Miss Millette:

"According to the arrangements agreed upon, I am enclosing a money order for $160, due on May 14.

"Mr. Bern has already left on his vacation, but I am at the office in the meantime, and if I can help you in any way at any time please don't hesitate to ask me.

"I hope you are comfortably and happily settled in your new home.

Sincerely yours,
Irene Harrison,
Secretary to Mr. Bern."

Jean Harlow's stepfather, Marino Bello, said she had known nothing about the "other woman," but this was contradicted by Paul's brother, Henry Bern, who said that everyone had known about Miss Millette and that Paul had specifically discussed Miss Millette with Miss Harlow.

Barbara La Marr in her canoe car. Bern bought her a house and hired nurses to care for her.

The Museum of Modern Art/Film Stills Archive

The room in which Paul Bern ended his life. Jay Sebring, a victim in the Manson-Tate murders, was also to live in the rustic mansion. *Los Angeles Times Photo*

On September 6, the day after Bern died, Dorothy checked out of the Plaza Hotel and boarded the Sacramento riverboat *Delta King*. At 4:45 a.m. the deck officer found a woman's coat and shoes beside the railing. Miss Millette was not aboard when the boat arrived at Sacramento. Two weeks later her body was found in the river.

Less than a week later, Jean Harlow returned to work on *Red Dust,* with Clark Gable.

Exactly a year later, in September, 1933, Jean eloped to Yuma, Arizona, and was married to Harold G. Rosson, a $1,200-a-week MGM cameraman, by a justice of the peace. They separated less than eight months later.

The Bern case seemed far in the past.

Then, in 1934, a new grand jury, investigating District Attorney Buron Fitts, obtained the records of the grand jury that had looked into Bern's death. The new grand jury said it was only interested in Fitts' expenditures for the grand jury.

But Fitts took the offensive, releasing some of the testimony before the 1932 grand jury. The most important revelations were in the testimony of Davis, the gardener, and Miss Harrison, the secretary.

"I think it was murder," said Davis. "I thought so from the beginning."

He said Carmichael, the butler, had "lied" about the tragedy. "He said they did not have a fuss the night before Bern's death. He said they got along fine. He said he had never heard anything about turning the place over to Bern's mother, when he had.

"He said Bern and Miss Harlow were hugging and kissing all the time, and Bern was talking of committing suicide, when really they didn't do much hugging and kissing, and Bern never did say anything about committing suicide."

Miss Harrison said that Jean Harlow had been the suitor, not Bern, during the courtship that preceded their marriage, and that Bern "didn't look particularly happy at the reception" that followed the ceremony.

A question that led to all sorts of interesting speculation had been asked of Garrison, the chauffeur:

"Did you hear about the time Mr. Bern found his wife in the hotel here?"

Garrison swore he hadn't. He also said no when asked if he had "ever seen Miss Harlow out with anyone but Bern."

Davis said the supposed suicide note was not in Bern's handwriting.

But the most sensational testimony given to the first grand jury was that a strange woman who avoided the servants had spent a good deal of time with Bern on that Sunday evening, his last night alive. Winifred Carmichael, the cook, reluctantly told of hearing a woman's voice, which was unfamiliar to her, in the house. The woman screamed once. Later Mrs. Carmichael found a woman's swimsuit, wet, on the edge of Bern's private swimming pool. On a table nearby were two empty glasses.

The following morning, according to Davis, the gardener, there was broken glass and a small puddle of blood near Bern's favorite chair by the swimming pool.

Davis had told all this to the police, who made no move to follow up these promising leads. But after the gardener was questioned by the police, he was summoned by telephone to the Bello home. There, Davis said, Jean Harlow's stepfather said to him, "You are talking too much. Move your wife and family over to the garage and keep your damned mouth shut."

Bern had not liked Bello, according to Davis, "and Bello did not like Bern."

A further mystery was introduced into the case when it was later learned that Miss Harlow had made a secret visit to San Francisco a few days before Bern's death.

Had she kept a rendezvous there with Dorothy Millette?

She insisted that she had not seen Dorothy. Nevertheless, the rumors grew. As Bosley Crowther recalled in his superb biography of Louis B. Mayer, *Hollywood Rajah,* "There were those who had strong suspicions that [Miss Harlow] had been involved in a plot of some sort against her husband with his former common-law wife."

For a time MGM feared "a threatened indictment of Miss Harlow on a murder charge." But studio boss Mayer, exerting all of his great political influence behind the scenes, was able to ward off that threat.

Officially, the Bern death was still a suicide.

During the next three years Miss Harlow's favorite escort was actor William Powell, who appeared to be deeply in love with her.

In 1936 Jean's health began to deteriorate. She suffered

such a severe sunburn that she was forced to postpone work for several weeks and undergo special medical treatment. Then came a serious throat infection. Weakened by these illnesses, she fell prey to influenza that winter. As winter waned and spring began, she was on the sick list a large part of the time with bad colds. Then her gallbladder became inflamed. Uremic poisoning developed.

After a week in Good Samaritan Hospital, Jean Harlow—with her mother, stepfather, a cousin and Powell at her bedside—died of cerebral edema. She was twenty-six.

Twenty-three years later there was another brief flurry of interest in the case. Screenwriter Ben Hecht, in the November 1960 issue of *Playboy* magazine, wrote, "Paul Bern, remembered for having committed suicide as the impotent bridegroom of Jean Harlow, the great cinema sexpot, did no such thing. His suicide note, hinting that he was sexually incompetent and had therefore 'ended the comedy', was a forgery. Studio officials decided, sitting in a conference around his dead body, that it was better to have Paul dead as a suicide than as the murder victim of another woman. It would be less a black eye for their biggest movie-making heroine, La Belle Harlow. It might crimp her box-office allure to have her blazoned as a wife who couldn't hold her husband."

The Los Angeles district attorney got in touch with Hecht, who told him that director Henry Hathaway had told him about the tragedy. But Hathaway, who was living in Nyack, New York, by then, said he had no firsthand knowledge of the case. As far as he knew, the suicide note was not a forgery.

And there the mystery remains.

If Bern really did kill himself, the Hollywood big shots who suppressed (and possibly faked) evidence, threw political influence in the way of a real police investigation, and otherwise did their best to hide the facts were guilty of incredible stupidity. The suicide of Jean Harlow's husband wouldn't necessarily have reflected on her attractiveness as a woman.

These considerations lend weight to the suspicion that Bern was murdered, and that the studio bosses knew it and faked the evidence to hide the crime.

But if he was murdered, who murdered him?

Dorothy Millette? Perhaps. She had written something on a pad in her hotel room. Only one word could be identified from the impressions on the paper underneath. The word was

Mr. and Mrs. Will Hays with Norma Shearer and Irving Thalberg, who had danced at the wedding. Did the studio push ''suicide-for-impotence'' to take the heat off their sex goddess?

The Museum of Modern Art/Film Stills Archive

"justification." It isn't difficult to build a whole murder theory around that word and Dorothy's past history. Had she been so shattered by Bern's marriage that she had immediately begun to make plans to kill him?

But if Dorothy Millette had killed Bern in Los Angeles on Sunday night, why did she bother to go back to the hotel in San Francisco, pack her things, check out, board the river-boat, and then commit suicide? Wouldn't she have been more likely to kill herself right after she killed Bern?

The only answer to that question is that she was irrational. It is not a very satisfactory answer.

Did Jean Harlow have a secret meeting with Dorothy Millette in San Francisco a few days before Bern's death? If the answer to that question is yes, then this whole fantastic case becomes wilder than Hollywood's most absurd thrillers.

5 Thelma Todd:
The Wrong Time For Death

It's interesting to conjecture what might have become of Thelma Todd if she had not gone into motion pictures. The daughter of a Lawrence, Massachusetts, politician named John Shaw Todd, she grew up to be a beautiful blonde with the kind of figure that dazed men. As a teenager she won a beauty contest that earned her the title of "Miss Massachusetts." She had decided to be a schoolteacher, and she earned some of her tuition at normal school by working as a fashion model.

One can picture her becoming a teacher, marrying a promising young local man after a few years, and becoming the vivacious, party-loving life of the country club, hated by all the other women and secretly desired by all the men.

Instead, her life was changed by a local theater manager who knew her father. The theater man sent the girl's photograph to Jesse Lasky, with a letter urging that producer to give her a job. Lasky decided to enter her in the first class of a school for young actors that he had persuaded his studio, Paramount, to establish at its eastern studios at Astoria, Queens.

The ex-beauty queen was one of the few stars who managed the switch from silents to talkies. She worked in comedies with all the biggies, including Laurel and Hardy and the Marx Brothers.

Eddie Brandt's Saturday Matinee

Thelma Todd gave up teaching the sixth grade when
Jesse Lasky invited her to Paramount's acting school.
She made over seventy movies.

Eddie Brandt's Saturday Matinee

Lasky's letter arrived at the Todd house shortly after Thelma began her first term as a sixth-grade teacher. She threw up the job at once and headed for New York City. For six months she, and twenty-three other young men and women, studied dramatics, make-up, costuming, etiquette, riding, fencing, dancing, swimming, and auto driving. On March 2, 1926, a graduation dinner was held at the Ritz-Carlton Hotel, and Thelma and fifteen others who had shown promise got one-year contracts with options. The sixteen youngsters appeared in a film, *Fascinating Youth,* which had parts written especially for each of them; it did fairly well. Only one other actor trained in the short-lived school ever really became a big Hollywood name; that was Charles (Buddy) Rogers, who eventually married Mary Pickford.

Thelma Todd appeared in a number of silent films and was one of those actresses who successfully made the transition from silents to talkies. She was the all-round actress; she appeared in Westerns, comedies, musicals, mysteries, melodramas, and serious drama. Her forte was comedy, however, as she showed in assignments with the Marx Brothers and with Laurel and Hardy. She appeared as a comedy team with Patsy Kelly in a series of remarkably funny two-reelers. By the time of her death, when she was a mere thirty years old, she had made more than seventy movies.

She was a healthy, happy-looking girl, full of bouncing vitality. But like many girls of her type, she concealed a heart that was Gothic. Occasionally her close friends would catch a momentary glimpse of that inner self, full of brooding doubts, gloom, and unhappiness. "Life isn't worth the candle," she once muttered to a friend. "While we're here we should laugh, be gay, and have fun."

Thelma Todd laughed, was gay, had fun. She acquired a reputation for practical jokes without malice. She was a fixture at parties. Her love affairs were many and often casual.

In July 1932, Thelma eloped to Prescott, Arizona, with Pasquale (Pat) Di Cicco, an actor's agent. Later they dropped in on a minister in Los Angeles and renewed their vows before him. But neither the civil nor the religious bonds held; on March 3, 1934, Miss Todd obtained a divorce from Di Cicco, charging cruelty and incompatibility.

By now she was beginning to think of the future. She had lasted eight years in Hollywood, and she knew that most stars had a fairly short career. She didn't want to end up destitute. So she invested some of her money in a beach restaurant on the coast highway north of Santa Monica. Her partner in the venture was Roland West, a former director. She and West maintained separate apartments on the second floor over the restaurant; apparently the relationship was purely business, despite rumors to the contrary. West also had a bungalow high on the hill above the restaurant, and attached to the bungalow was a two-car garage where Thelma kept her car.

The restaurant was profitable, and the money kept rolling in from the Todd pictures, as she continued as much in demand for new roles as ever. But life was becoming complicated for Thelma Todd. She became a target for extortion threats, and at least one man was arrested for trying to shake her down. It was rumored that blackmailers were plaguing her, too. Sometimes she would ask her chauffeur to drive faster because she was afraid some "gangsters" might try to kidnap her. What all this meant, nobody seemed to know after her death, or if they knew, they weren't going to say.

Early in December 1935, Stanley Lupino, the comedian, and his daughter, Ida, who would later be recognized as one of the greatest talents in Hollywood, decided to give a party in honor of Thelma. It was to be held at the Trocadero restaurant. A few days before the party, Ida Lupino chanced to meet Di Cicco, who asked why she hadn't invited him to the party.

"I thought it might be embarrassing for you and Thelma," Miss Lupino said.

"I'd like to come," Di Cicco told her. So she invited him.

On the night of the party, a seat was left vacant beside Thelma for Di Cicco. But when he arrived at the restaurant, an actress on his arm, the two went to a table in another part of the restaurant.

"He and Thelma spoke," Miss Lupino said later, "but she was very indignant. She berated him bitterly for slighting me and herself."

It was, according to one witness, "a terrific argument."

A few hours later Thelma Todd left the party, apparently in a gay mood. Before she got into her limousine, in front of the Troc, she turned, made an exaggerated wave of salute to her friends, and cried out with mock solemnity, "Goodbye!"

Later her friends were to wonder whether she had been more serious than they imagined at that moment.

Ida Lupino's family threw the last party Thelma ever
went to and invited Thelma's ex-, Pat Di Cicco.

The Museum of Modern Art/Film Stills Archive

As Miss Todd was driven home in a rented car, she again asked the driver, Ernest O. Peters, to drive faster because she was afraid she might be slain or kidnapped by gangsters.

Sometime about 4 a.m.—give or take a half hour—Peters brought the car to a stop in front of Miss Todd's restaurant. It was his custom to see her to the top of the stairs to her apartment, but on this night she told him that it wouldn't be necessary. She was still on the sidewalk when he drove off. It was then early Sunday morning.

She was never seen alive again.

On Monday morning Thelma Todd's maid reported for work. Puzzled at not finding her mistress in the apartment, she looked up the hill and noticed one of the doors of the garage partly open. So she wearily climbed the 270 steps to the garage, pushed the door open, and went to Miss Todd's car.

She found Thelma slumped in the driver's seat, with blood on her face. There was blood on the seat and on the runningboard of the car, too. But Miss Todd was still wearing her evening gown and fur jacket, and they had not been torn or otherwise disturbed. And her hands and long fingernails bore no sign of a struggle.

When the police arrived, shortly after 10:30 that morning, they set to work with a will. But almost immediately the power of the motion picture industry was brought to bear, as it always has been in Hollywood scandals.

To the first police on the case, to Thelma's mother, to many of the grand jurors, and to most of the correspondents, it looked like murder. But before the next few hours and days were out, the police were calling it suicide; Mrs. Todd was calling it an accident, and it was obvious that a real murder investigation—with its inevitable airing of dirty linen—would not be permitted.

So from this point on, we cannot speak of facts as such. All we can say is that these were officially reported to be facts.

The autopsy showed that carbon monoxide poisoning from the auto exhaust was the cause of death. The face was bruised, but the police insisted that she had banged it against the steering wheel when she collapsed. Those who regarded the death as murder pointed out that someone could have struck her in the face, then placed her unconscious body in the car and started the motor. All the evidence was consistent with such a theory.

Thelma Todd's Sidewalk Cafe. The steps up the hill lead to the garage where Thelma kept her car, next to West's bungalow. *Charles Rhodes for Fawcett Publications*

Adolph Zukor and Jesse Lasky, no strangers to silencing scandals. It was Lasky who brought Thelma to Hollywood. *Copyright 1938 Paramount Pictures Inc*

The accident theory was based on the assumption that Miss Todd had forgotten to take the key to her apartment. Finding herself locked out in the pre-dawn chill, she had climbed the hill to the garage, had rested in the car, and had turned on the motor to keep warm. But her evening slippers were not scuffed, and in a test climb of the same stone steps it was found that such slippers would be badly scuffed.

That meant that Thelma had not walked to the garage; she had driven there. But how could that be, when Peters had deposited her on the sidewalk far below?

Then it became apparent that all of the assumptions about the case were wrong in one of their basic premises. Thelma Todd had not died early Sunday morning; she had died late Sunday night or early Monday morning!

There seemed to be no doubt about it. The autopsy disclosed food that Miss Todd had eaten somewhere, some time after the Troc party. Mrs. Wallace Ford said she'd had a telephone call from Thelma at 4 p.m. Sunday to say she'd be at Mrs. Ford's cocktail party that afternoon, and "when you see who's coming with me, you'll drop dead!" (Miss Todd, of course, did not attend the party.) A druggist and one of his customers told of seeing a blonde in evening gown and fur jacket, whom they identified positively as Thelma Todd, make a telephone call from a booth in the drugstore about the time Mrs. Ford got her call. At 11 p.m. Sunday, less than twelve hours before Miss Todd's body was found, a woman answering her description went into a tobacco shop and asked the proprietor to make a phone call to a number that ended in "7771." Before he could make the call, however, she ran out and went down the street to meet a man who was holding a woman's fur jacket.

And it was about that time Sunday night that Jewel Carmen, the estranged wife of Thelma Todd's partner, West, passed a car containing Miss Todd and a man she didn't recognize. Miss Carmen, a former silent movie actress, knew Miss Todd very well; there was no question about her identification.

All of the new witnesses identified the strange man as "dark and foreign-looking." He was never found.

The investigation turned to Thelma's love life. She had told her friends about a new man in her life who couldn't attend the party at the Troc because he was in San Francisco, but she had not named the man. There was Di Cicco, who had been her husband; he insisted that everything had been pleasant

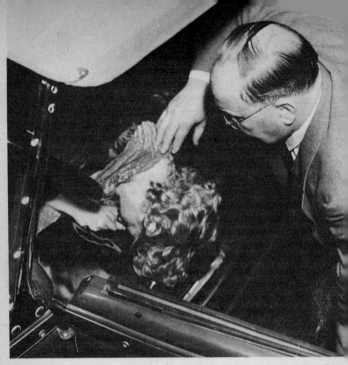

Thelma Todd's body is examined by the Los Angeles Police. Death was attributed to carbon monoxide poisoning, but there were clues pointing in other directions. *Wide World Photos*

between them, and he didn't mention the row at the Troc. There were other men.

During the Lupino party, Miss Todd had gone over to a table in the nightclub where theater owner Sid Grauman was sitting with three other men. When she returned to her party, she seemed downcast. The reason was never satisfactorily explained.

In the end, the coroner's jury decided the death was probably accidental, and so did Thelma's mother.

Deputy District Attorney George Johnson didn't agree. "It seems too difficult to believe Miss Todd went to that garage and started the motor of her car to keep warm," he said. He thought it was suicide, despite the absence of note or known motive.

But Patsy Kelly, one of Thelma's closest friends, asserted, "Thelma would not kill herself. She had every reason to live, none to die." And the grand jury foreman grumbled, "It looks as if they're trying to build up this case as a suicide, but in the actual evidence, I have found nothing to support this theory definitely."

Miss Todd's lawyer said flatly that he thought she'd been murdered.

Nearly three months later a middle-aged, well-dressed, black-haired woman sent a telegram from Ogden, Utah, to the Los Angeles Police Department. She said the man who "killed Thelma Todd" was in Ogden. The telegram gave his name and that of the Ogden hotel in which he had been living since January, that is, since immediately after the death.

The Los Angeles police did not make the telegram public, but the Ogden police, who were obviously on their toes, found out about the telegram and the woman, and conducted a quiet investigation. Then the mayor, Harmon Peery, and Police Chief Rial Moore notified the Los Angeles cops of their findings. "Someone should question the man who has been located," the mayor said.

But nobody did. The Los Angeles cops sent word to Ogden that the Todd case was closed. As far as they were concerned, it was suicide.

Hollywood's secrets once again had been protected.

6 Mary Astor:
The Trouble with Diaries

"Never eat at a place called 'Mom's'; never play pool with a man called Pops; and never go to bed with anyone who's got more troubles than you do."

Although that bit of unconventional advice has been credited to many people, it is generally believed that the author was George S. Kaufman, long-time drama editor of the *New York Times,* Pulitzer Prize-winning playwright (twice), occasional screenwriter, director, celebrated cynic, and for many years one of America's most quoted wits.

But he didn't always follow his own advice.

For example, when he began a love affair with film star Mary Astor, she had more troubles than he did.

Before events had run their course, he had more troubles than he had started out with, more than he really wanted. In fact, as a hypochondriac, he had no need of any troubles—he could always invent some if life grew dull.

Trouble entered the love affair of Mary Astor and George S. Kaufman because she kept a diary.

The habit of keeping a diary was one that Miss Astor picked

Lucille Langehanke was no name for an actress so Publicity came up with Mary Astor. She married a doctor and had a child, but her best friend was still her diary.

up from her mother, a Kansas farm girl who had married a German immigrant, Otto Ludwig Wilhelm Langehanke. He earned a meager living teaching German and working in department stores. On May 3, 1906, the only child they would ever have, Lucile (with two l's instead of the usual three), was born in Quincy, Illinois, where Otto was teaching in a high school.

While Lucile was still a pre-teen girl, her father got the idea that she should become a movie actress. Motion pictures were growing increasingly popular throughout the country, and the Langehankes were confirmed fans. In order to further his ambitions for his daughter, Langehanke moved the family in 1920 to New York, which was still a major film-making center. There the fifteen-year-old girl, already a striking beauty, was signed to a contract by Famous Players-Lasky after she and her parents had met with Jesse Lasky, director Walter Wanger, and movie columnist Louella O. Parsons. The studio felt strongly that Lucile Langehanke was no name for a movie actress, so the publicity department came up with a new name: Mary Astor.

In 1923 the family moved to Hollywood. After performing in two insignificant motion pictures, she was "lent out," as the phrase went—"rented out" would be more accurate—by her studio to Warner Brothers. The great John Barrymore had asked for her to play against him in *Beau Brummel*.

She was just seventeen, and he was forty, but he became her first lover.

It wasn't easy. Mary was making a great deal of money now, but she wasn't permitted by her parents to keep a penny of it. (After a brief revolt a little later she was given $5 a week "pin money.") She was never alone; one or both parents was always with her. Even on the set, her mother was an ever-vigilant chaperone. Whenever Mary's off-camera conversation with anyone was prolonged, her mother would plunge into the talk. If Mary went to the rest room, her mother tagged along.

The girl was, in effect, a prisoner.

The resourceful Barrymore found a way around the parental watchdogs. He told her parents that she didn't know enough about acting, but he'd be willing to coach her. After a few teaching sessions in the Langehanke living room, with father and mother listening in the dining room, Barrymore told them he had to be completely alone with their daughter. She was too self-conscious, too inhibited by the knowledge that they were listening. Guessing that they had some misgivings about his intentions, he told them, "Don't be ridiculous. This is a *kid!*"

Although they were almost paranoid in their suspicions of everyone, the parents somehow accepted Barrymore's argument. From then on, every Sunday Mary's mother would sit on the veranda of the Beverly Hills Hotel, sewing, while inside, in Barrymore's suite, her daughter and the famous actor were making love.

Nevertheless, the affair was much more than a matter of sexual satisfaction. Mary was overwhelmingly in love with Barrymore, and there is considerable evidence that his own feelings were just as profound. But she was unwilling to complete the process of growing up by breaking free of her parents' suffocating presence and by accepting the responsibilities and demands of life as an independent adult, so the romance ultimately ended. Whether Barrymore's future would have been different if Mary had been willing to break free for him, no one can know. He himself told her, about 1938, "It's a good thing I wasn't free to marry [then]. And it's a good thing I couldn't get you away from your family. I would have married you, and you would have had a miserable life." But Mary thought it might have worked out otherwise. He seemed at peace with himself during their affair. He drank very little during that time. But in the years that followed he drank more and more, until, long before his death in 1942, "The Great Profile," as he was called, was incapable of working in anything but "inferior comedies caricaturing his own debauchery and alcoholism," as *The Filmgoer's Companion* put it succinctly.

By 1928 Mary Astor was earning $3,750 a week from William Fox; she was a well-established star. But the talkies were coming in, and Fox had some reservations about how Mary would sound as she spoke her lines. A contract row between the studio and her father, who still managed her business affairs and took most of her money, ended in the studio's refusal to renew her contract and in a decision by the producers' association that none of its members would deal with the elder Langehanke.

After a successful stage appearance—which proved the strength of her voice—Mary Astor again was in demand for screen roles. Things were looking up for her in 1929 when her

She was just seventeen and he was forty when John Barrymore became Mary's first lover. First the resourceful Barrymore had to find a way around Mary's wary parents. *The Museum of Modern Art / Film Stills Archive*

life suddenly fell apart again: her husband of less than a year, director Kenneth Hawks, was killed when an airplane in which he was flying for some aerial sequences collided with another plane being flown in the same movie.

Gradually she picked up the pieces of her life. She began to work again in talking pictures. She came out of her shell a bit and met people. Eventually actor Lee Tracy introduced her to a friend of his, Dr. Franklyn Thorpe. Months later, on June 29, 1931, she married the doctor. A year later, Mary gave birth to a three-pound, six-ounce baby, Marylyn.

Before long, it was obvious that the marriage wasn't working out very well. The couple talked divorce, but put off action for the time being.

Pressed for money, Mary gave up her one-third interest in the estate her father had bought with her money, but she informed her parents that they would get no more money from her, at least, not on a regular basis. Their response was to file suit against her for support. The suit was dismissed when she told the court she would be willing to pay $100 a month toward her parents' maintenance.

In May 1933, between pictures, she flew to New York. There, through mutual friends, she met George S. Kaufman. It was a meeting destined to embarrass both of them. They fell in love. And Mary confided the entire story to her diary.

"I had realized for some time that it [the diary] might be used in a divorce action," Miss Astor recalled in her autobiography, *My Story*. Nevertheless, she was astonishingly casual about hiding it from her husband. It contained specific, detailed information about Kaufman, about her previous lovers, and about other people who had confided their secrets to Mary. When Mary told her husband that she had rented a small house, that she was moving out with the baby, he disclosed that he had taken the diary. If there were to be a custody fight, he would make its contents public, in an effort to persuade the court that Mary was unfit to be given custody of Marylyn.

When the lawyers were done, it was agreed that Mary would have actual custody of the baby, but Dr. Thorpe would get legal custody. Later that year, 1935, the doctor got an uncontested divorce.

A year later an actress friend urged Mary to get in touch with attorney Roland Rich Woolley, to see if he couldn't do something about that legal custody problem. When she did consult the lawyer, he said he thought there was a good chance that he could keep the diary out of evidence. So Mary sued for custody.

And all hell broke loose.

The lawyer, as it turned out, was right: he was able to prevent the diary from being entered as evidence, for technical reasons.

But parts of the diary were leaked to the press, which published the excerpts with great glee. "I fell like a ton of bricks—as only I can fall," she was quoted as having written.

The first day they were together Kaufman took her to the Casino for lunch. That evening they "sneaked into the Music Box where his show *Of Thee I Sing* was playing." The next day, a Sunday, they had dinner together, saw a movie, and "laughed a lot and liked each other even more." Monday was "very hot and we got a cab and drove around the park a few times and the park was—well, the park—and he held my hand and said he'd like to kiss me but didn't. . . ."

Tuesday was The Night. They had dinner at Twenty-One, the exclusive night spot, and went to a play: "I don't think either of us remember much what the show was about."

According to a privately distributed account, which could not be printed in newspapers or magazines because of editorial restrictions at the time, the diary at that point went on: "We played kneesies during the first two acts. . . . My hand wasn't in my own hand during the third [act]. . . . It's been years since I've felt up a man in public, but I just got carried away. . . ."

After the show they had a drink someplace and "then went to a little flat on 73rd Street where we could be alone and it was all very thrilling and beautiful."

At that point, the privately circulated version said: "Once George lays down his glasses, he is *quite* a different man. His powers of recuperation are amazing, and we made love all night. . . . It all worked perfectly, and we shared our fourth climax at dawn.

"I didn't see much of anybody else the rest of the time; we saw every show in town, had grand fun together, and went frequently to 73rd Street, where he fucked the living daylights out of me. . . .

"I remember one morning about 4:00 we had a sandwich at Reuben's, and it was just getting daylight, so we drove through the park in an open cab, and the street lights went out, and the birds started singing, and it was cool and dewy and pretty heavenly, and heavenly, too, to pet and French . . . right out in the open. . . .

"Was any woman ever happier? It seems that George is just hard all the time. . . . I have never known such a thrilling ecstacy. He fits me perfectly. . . . Oh, so many exquisite moments—twenty, count them diary, twenty! . . . . I don't see how he does it. . . . He is perfect."

Of a tryst at Palm Springs, the diary allegedly said: "Ah, desert night—with George's body plunging into mine, naked under the stars. . . ."

Not the sort of thing one would want a spouse to read. Definitely not.

Yet the diary apparently was just tossed carelessly into a dresser drawer, where Dr. Thorpe, her estranged and probably suspicious mate, predictably found it. Dr. Thorpe didn't tell his wife what he had discovered. But he did take action, as another diary entry in 1935, when Kaufman was in Hollywood to write *A Night at the Opera* for the Marx Brothers, shows:

"I called for George at the Beverly-Wilshire at seven. He was very pleasant but a little jittery and strained, I noticed. In the car on the way to the Trocadero, I said, 'Feeling lowish?'

" 'Mm—yeah—I'll tell you about it.'

"We went downstairs to the bar, sat down at the table, and ordered drinks.

" 'Shall I wait for you to have a drink [Kaufman rarely drank] or shall I plunge right in?'

"I was pretty mystified and worried, and said, 'Plunge in, I'm dying of curiosity.'

" 'I've had a visit from your husband,' [he said]. I practically went through the floor.

"Franklyn [had] called on him about 11 o'clock Sunday morning. They talked for about half an hour in which Franklyn stated the reason for his visit, shook hands, and parted—all very pleasantly.

"He told George that he knew that he could not completely fulfill my life, that I needed other interests, but the sacredness of marriage, the child was at stake, and George must be willing to take his share of the responsibility involved. What he meant by that, specifically, or what he wanted George to do, exactly, George couldn't find out.

"What he expected to gain from the interview is more than I can figure. He doesn't know yet that I know about it. It seems to me that probably in all honesty he loves me and wants to keep me at all costs and probably wanted to frighten George into breaking off with me.

"I told George that if he wanted to get out, he could. His answer was very nice: "I'll have no farewell scenes with you, Miss A. I don't want that.""

Mary Astor was only one of scores of women with whom Kaufman dallied during his seventy-two years of life; and it was true, he had never liked farewell scenes. Farewells, yes; farewell *scenes,* no.

As soon as he could, Kaufman fled back to New York, where he told his wife, Beatrice, all about the trouble he was in. She was very understanding. For most of their eighteen years of marriage she, as well as he, had engaged in extramarital activities. She predicted that it would all blow over.

For a year it appeared that she was right. Kaufman went out to Hollywood again to collaborate with Moss Hart on the play, *You Can't Take It with You,* which would win the Pulitzer Prize and later, when it was made into a film, the Academy Award. Mary Astor's suit against her ex-husband came to trial while Kaufman was in California. Inevitably, Dr. Thorpe's lawyers served Kaufman with a subpoena to appear as a witness. When the day came, Kaufman did not show up in court, and a bench warrant was issued for him.

Fleeing the minions of the law, Kaufman slipped out of the Beverly-Wilshire Hotel, made his way to Moss Hart's house, again gave the sheriff's deputies the dodge and got aboard the yacht of Irving Thalberg and Norma Shearer. With the deputies in close pursuit, Kaufman disembarked at Catalina Island, got back on the yacht, returned to Hart's residence. When the deputies rang the front doorbell, Kaufman skittered out the back door and hid in some bushes nearby. Finally he escaped from California disguised as a medical patient, his face hidden by bandages and his body wrapped in blankets, aboard an eastbound train.

By that time, the excerpts from the diary had caused the newspapers to label Kaufman "Public Lover No. 1"—despite his ungainly body, his thick glasses, his big nose, and his generally unimpressive overall appearance. There were screaming black headlines on the front pages of every news-paper in the country, including Kaufman's own working home, the *New York Times.* Under great pressure from their editors, the reporters laid siege to Kaufman's town house at 14

George S. Kaufman with Rupert Hughes. "Once George lays down his glasses, he is quite a different man," wrote Mary. ". . . he fucked the living daylights out of me." *The Museum of Modern Art / Film Stills Archive*

Dr. Franklyn Thorpe, Judge Goodwin J. Knight, Mary Astor, and 4-year-old Marilyn pose for the cameras during the custody trial. *Evening News*

East 94th Street in New York. On August 14, 1936, he finally opened the door and invited his fellow journalists in for a press conference.

Clearly nervous, Kaufman's famed wit failed him that day. The best he could come up with was this:

"I have one piece of news for the Great American Public: I do *not* keep a diary myself."

His wife was in Europe when the scandal hit the front pages. As she boarded ship in England, on her way home, she told the reporters: "I knew all about this case before it caught the limelight. I know Mary Astor. I know her well [that wasn't true]. . . . They had a flirtation. I can't see there's any terrible harm in that. . . .

"We have been married twenty years. We are adults, leading our lives in adult fashion. George is a good husband. I love him very much. He is in love with me despite the things that may have happened. . . .

"She kept a diary. Very stupid, that."

On her arrival in New York, Mrs. Kaufman made her position crystal clear.

"Young actresses," she told the ship reporters, "are an occupational hazard for any man working in the theater."

The only long-term effects of the scandal on Kaufman were his greatly increased devotion (but not fidelity) to his wife and their purchase of a country retreat—Barley Sheaf Farm, near Holicong, in Bucks County, Pennsylvania—where they could escape some of the New York gossip. Eventually Kaufman went back to Los Angeles, apologized to the judge for having disobeyed the subpoena, and paid a $500 fine.

Mary Astor's career was not hurt by the affair. She had just completed *Dodsworth* when the diary hit the headlines, and audiences stood and cheered when she appeared on screen in it. Although she had feared the furor might put an end to her career—she had even made plans to go to work as a buyer for an exclusive women's wear store—the studios decided there was no necessity to invoke the morality clause in her contract. Samuel Goldwyn may have tipped the scales when he said, "A woman fighting for her child? This is good!"

Well into the 1960s she continued to be in demand for motion pictures and television. In 1941 she won an Oscar as Best Supporting Actress for her work in *The Great Lie*.

But the trauma of the trial—on top of the repressive,

crippling discipline of her childhood and early adult years—
took its toll of her spirit.

"[I was] sick, spoiled, selfish, prowling like some jungle
animal seeking momentary satisfaction," she wrote many
years later in *My Story*. "Sexually I was out of control. I was
drinking too much, and I was brought up short when I found
myself late in the evening thinking someone was 'terribly
attractive' and wondering the next morning, 'Why, why!'"

In those words, she was too harsh on herself. Probably she
had always judged herself too pitilessly. Her behavior certainly was not conspicuously worse than that of millions of
other basically good people, in and out of Hollywood.

Besides keeping up an active, productive work life, she
overcame depression that led to attempted suicide, and she
conquered alcoholism.

Although she herself never completed high school, because of her acting career, she has written two volumes of
autobiography and five novels, all of them well-written, displaying the sensitivity, innate elegance, and grace that made
her such a great actress.

In the 1970s she was living at the Motion Picture Country
Home at Woodland Hills, California. She was responsible
there for the Motion Picture and Television Fund, which
provides assistance to elderly actors and actresses.

But she still insisted that many of the excerpts from her
diary published in the newspapers forty years earlier were
fictitious. But there had been a diary, she conceded, and
some of the less explicit passages were accurate, as printed
in the press.

What she still didn't seem to realize was that it really didn't
matter. The only thing that counted was that a great actress
had confronted a crisis of public opinion courageously—and
won.

7 Errol Flynn:
The Moon Through a Porthole

There were always girls in Errol Flynn's life; lots of girls. And he liked 'em young, which was unfortunate. Because one girl met him at a party, and another girl went for a sail on his yacht, and then both of them cried, *Rape!*

And so a phrase was born.

"I'm in like Flynn."

He was the son of a marine biologist who settled in Tasmania after the baby was born there. They christened him Errol Leslie Thomson Flynn. As a boy he was stuck in a boarding school in London and all but forgotten—or so he felt—by his family. He rebelled against all authority; the school expelled him. Then another school expelled him. Next came a school in Australia. Then a period knocking about the South Sea Islands. . . . All manner of odd bits, until finally he made his way to London, spent a year and a half with a repertory group. After that, a small part in a film, *Murder at Monte Carlo,* produced by Warner Brothers as a quickie in England. Jack Warner spotted the handsome, debonair young Irishman in the movie and offered him a six-month contract at one hundred and fifty dollars a week.

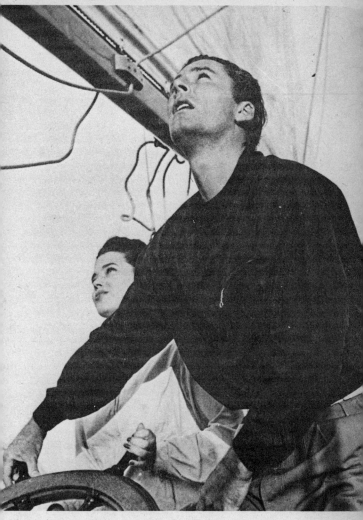

This picture of the "rapist" and his victim on board the Sirocco was introduced as evidence. She saw the moon through a porthole—on the wrong side of the boat.
Wide World Photos

Almost immediately, Flynn became a star, to many moviegoers the greatest swashbuckler of them all, especially as *Captain Blood*.

He became famous as a man-about-Hollywood, a bon vivant, a connoisseur of fine woman-flesh, a man who violated the biblical injunction against looking upon the wine when it is red—who violated a good many other biblical injunctions, too.

Then, late one night in 1942, two plainclothesmen called on Errol Flynn and told him, "We have a very serious charge against you."

They told him the story: a girl named Betty Hansen had come from Nebraska to visit her sister in Los Angeles. In due course she was missing and the cops were asked to look for her; she hadn't been home for a few days. Betty was found in a hotel in Santa Monica. The police took her in, began questioning her. She began to tell them about her adventures, which turned out to be mainly sexual. One of the men she named was Errol Flynn. To back up her story, she also produced his unlisted telephone number.

At this point, the cops might have been expected to call the District Attorney's office, which would then have put in a quick telephone call to the appropriate executives in the motion picture industry, and the usual cover-up would have taken place. But there was a new D.A. in office . . .

And so Flynn was made the scapegoat.

Betty Hansen, who claimed to be seventeen—below the age of consent—was taken before a grand jury, but that body, after questioning her, indicated how much weight it put in her testimony by refusing to indict Flynn. Normally, that would have been the end of the matter.

But not this time. The D.A.'s men kept trying to find something to bolster the case against Flynn. They found that a woman named Satterlee had complained to the sheriff's office about Flynn a year earlier. Mrs. Satterlee had asserted that Flynn had seduced her fifteen-year-old daughter, Peggy, aboard his yacht. The sheriff's men had looked into the charge but decided there was no case.

Now the D.A.'s office picked it up, dusted it off, and lumped it with the Hansen charge in a single District Attorney's complaint charging four counts of statutory rape.

Errol Flynn, the great lover, faced the prospect of at least five years in prison for being too loving off-screen.

Flynn's lawyer, Robert Ford, put in an SOS for that great

criminal lawyer, Jerry Giesler. He quickly ascertained the essential allegations regarding each girl.

Peggy Satterlee had accepted Flynn's invitation to go for a weekend sail aboard his yacht, the *Sirocco,* off Catalina Island, at the beginning of August 1941. They were not alone. Others aboard were Buster Wiles, a friend of Flynn; another girl; Peter Stackpole, the magazine photographer; and a crew of three. Flynn allegedly had intercourse with her twice: once early Sunday morning after returning to the yacht from spending Saturday evening ashore, and again Sunday night, as the yacht was nearing port. She had not complained to anyone aboard the yacht, and no one had been aware of the dastardly deed. She had even posed, smiling, for photographs with Flynn. The photos showed no scratches or bruises on either of them.

Betty Hansen had attended a party toward the end of September 1942 with a new-found friend. The party was held in the Bel Air mansion owned by Colleen Moore, silent screen star, and rented by three bachelors, Bruce Cabot, Freddie McEvoy, and Stephen Raphael. Betty was introduced to Flynn and sat on his lap in the den. Then she stayed to dinner, along with some of the other guests. After dinner, Flynn took her upstairs to a bedroom, she said, stripped her, took off his own clothes, and had intercourse with her.

World-shaking events were happening at that time. The Allies landed a huge army in French North Africa, German troops entered Unoccupied France, the Russians began their great counteroffensive at Stalingrad which would, within two months, result in the surrender of an entire German army, and Admiral Darlan, Vichy Chief of State of North Africa, was assassinated.

But the Errol Flynn rape case was the banner headline on most American newspapers almost every day.

At the preliminary hearing, Betty Hansen was questioned by Deputy District Attorney Thomas W. Cochran. He led the girl up to the events that followed the dinner:

Q. Did you go any place with Mr. Flynn?
A. Yes.
Q. Where did you go?
A. Upstairs.
Q. Just before you went upstairs do you recall anything that was said by yourself or Mr. Flynn?

Peggy Satterlee (with bandage) and Betty Hansen during Errol Flynn's trial for statutory rape. The fate-
worse-than-death didn't dampen their spirits.

United Press International Photo

A. I don't recall what was said, but I know something was said.

Q. By whom?

A. Flynn.

Q. What is your best recollection, if you have any recollection, as to what he did say to you?

A. I do not know the words, but that he was going to take me upstairs and lay me on the bed for a nap. . . .

Q. And when you got upstairs, where did you go?

A. The bedroom.

Q. Do you recall whether or not the door was locked or unlocked?

A. Locked.

Q. I mean before you got in?

A. It was unlocked.

Q. Was the door—did the door remain unlocked before you got in, or was some change made in it?

A. It was unlocked when we went in.

Q. After you got in?

A. It was unlocked.

Q. Was the door subsequently locked?

A. Yes.

Q. By whom?

A. Errol Flynn.

Q. All right now, after you got into this room, was anything said by Mr. Flynn to you or by you to Mr. Flynn?

A. Yes.

Q. Relate the conversation in full that you can now remember.

A. I believe he told me to lie down. . . .

Q. Tell the court what transpired from that time on, and what was said. Just go ahead, and relate what was done and said.

A. Well, Flynn took me in there and sat me down.

Q. Where?

A. On the twin bed, the first one.

Q. All right.

A. And I believe he told me to lie down, and I told him I did not want to take a nap, I could go back downstairs, and I do not know what he said or anything. He went out and locked the door and came back.

Q. Went and locked the door?

A. Yes.

Q. All right. Then what happened.

A. I had an act of intercourse.

Q. Before you had this act of intercourse, was anything done about your clothing or his?

A. Yes.

Q. Tell the court what was done in that respect.

A. He undressed me and then he got undressed.

Q. How were you dressed on that occasion?

A. I had slacks on.

Q. What else?

A. That is all.

Q. Did you have on panties?

A. Yes.

Q. When you say he undressed you, what of your clothing did he take off?

A. All of them.

Q. And of his clothing, what was taken off?

A. Everything except his shoes, I believe.

(Flynn's film, *They Died with Their Boots On*, had just been released. The testimony lent itself to all manner of bawdy jokes in every saloon in the country.)

On cross-examination, Giesler forced Betty to admit that she had gone to the party hoping to meet Flynn and that the fellow who took her there had told her to play up to Flynn in the hope he might help her get a job in motion pictures.

Then Giesler went on with his questioning:

Q. And in talking about playing up to Flynn, did he say anything about intercourse?

A. No, he did not.

Q. He did not mention intercourse at any time?

A. No, he did not.

Q. Now, then, for the purpose of refreshing your recollection, Miss Hansen, I will ask you, do you recall, do you remember your testimony you gave before the grand jury up on the fifth floor, or down on the fifth floor, of this building?

A. Yes.

Q. That was some little time ago?

A. Yes.

Q. I show you your testimony. . . . We are talking about Armand Knapp. That is the same young man?

A. Yes.

Q. [*reading*] "Did he say anything to you about going to introduce you to Errol Flynn? A. He said how I should act and play up to him. Q. Tell us about that. A. He said play up to him and drink with him and he even said to have intercourse with him." Do you remember so testifying? This is your—

A. No, I don't. . . .

Q. [*reading*] "Did Mr. Knapp tell you to have intercourse with Flynn? A. He said to be sociable and do anything he asked me to do." That is true?

A. Yes.

Later Giesler also brought the admission from Betty that she had told officers at the Juvenile Hall "that I undressed myself," contrary to her latest version.

A good deal of the Hansen testimony was wonderful fun.

Giesler asked Betty:

"When he told you to lie down on the bed, did he tell you what he wanted you to lie down for?"

"No, he did not," she replied.

"Did you have any thoughts of what he wanted you to lie down for?"

"No," she said, wide-eyed and innocent.

Then Giesler developed the fact that Betty had been surely one of the most cooperative rape victims on record, despite her assertions that she had resisted Flynn's blandishments.

Q. I believe you said you had some sport shirt?

A. Yes.

Q. Did that button or zip?

A. Buttoned.

Q. Did you help him on that?

A. I helped him.

Q. You did not know then what was going to happen?

A. No, I did not know exactly.

Q. What did you think was going to happen—just going to take a nap?

A. Yes.

Q. That is what you thought, and you were made more comfortable so that you could take a nap better?

A. Yes.

Q. And then you had on, I believe—in answer to Mr. Cochran's question I believe you used the word panties—you had some panties on?

A. Yes.

Q. How did they fasten, pull or zip? I do not know how they do. . . .

A. Just slip them on.

Q. You don't pull or zip?

A. No, they don't. . . .

Q. Did they have elastic band or not?

A. Yes.

Q. Were they tight around your waist?

A. Yes.

Q. Did you help take them off?

A. Not that I recall.

Q. May you have had to help take them off?

A. I might have.

Q. Did you still not know what was going to happen?

A. Maybe he took my clothes off to go to bed. Don't you take your clothes off to go to bed?

Q. Maybe I do. That is what you thought you went up there for?

A. Yes.

Q. When did you come to the conclusion that something was going to happen?

A. When he went and locked the door.

Q. Your clothes were off when he went to lock the door?

A. I believe they were.

Afterwards, she conceded, they got dressed and went downstairs, where Flynn kissed her and ''I kissed him back, I mean just one smack'' before he left the house.

Peggy Satterlee said she was lying in her bunk aboard the *Sirocco,* wearing only her slip in lieu of a nightgown, plus a pair of panties, when Flynn walked into her cabin.

''I said, 'You should not be here,' '' she testified, ''and he said 'I just want to talk to you,' and I said, 'You should not be here, because it is not nice to come in a lady's bedroom when she is in bed.' ''

Flynn pleaded with her to let him get in bed with her—''I just want to talk to you''—but she told him not ''to bother a nice girl,'' Peggy said. That apparently annoyed him, because he then told her, according to her testimony, ''I wanted to be nice to you, but you asked for it, so you will get it.''

And with that ''He just walked over to the bed, pulled down the covers and pulled up my slip and pulled down my pants.''

And then the villain possessed her.

Then came that part of Peggy's story that became most famous, the subject of more ribald amusement than any other part of what was to be a highly entertaining trial. This was the ''moon through the porthole'' incident.

Peggy said she was standing on the deck, commenting on the beauty of the moonlight, with Flynn.

Q. You referred to the moon, and he said it looked better from the porthole, did he?

A. Yes, sir.

Q. Did he carry you downstairs?

A. No, sir.

Q. Did he pull you downstairs?

A. No, sir.

Q. Did he then take hold of your arm and lead you downstairs?

A. He might have taken hold of my arm on the way down the steps, but I do not remember that he pulled me. . . .

Q. And you went in?

A. Into Mr. Wiles' room. . . .

Q. Why?

A. Because I wanted to see the moon through the porthole.

Peggy said the moon was on "the right side" of the boat.

As she looked through the porthole, she said, Flynn told her that since he'd enjoyed her once, there was no reason why he shouldn't partake again. She objected and tried to leave, but whenever she got up he pushed her back down on the bunk. She specifically said that she did not jump up on the bunk herself and that Flynn did not lift her up. These were to be important points.

Peggy told how she struggled on the bunk, trying to prevent Flynn from carrying out his naughty plans. She said she was on her side, wriggling constantly, kicking, fighting.

"And yet he completed the act?" Giesler asked with mild wonderment.

Peggy got flustered. She obviously had the same mental picture that was in every other mind in the courtroom. She asked permission to amplify her story.

"After I fought for a long time," she recalled, "he said, 'If you relax I won't hurt you,' and then I did."

The trial began early in January 1943 in the Superior Court of Los Angeles County. Betty Hansen was the first complaining witness to take the stand. She immediately added to Flynn's reputation for virility by declaring that the act of rape had taken "about fifty minutes."

Even Giesler was awed.

"And during the entire time he was on top of you?" he asked.

"That is right," she said.

Then Giesler forced Betty to admit that before the incident at the Bel Air house, she had been caught engaging in what Giesler called "some rather unusual sexual practices," which she had confessed before the grand jury. He pointed out that she was subject to a possible four-year sentence of imprisonment for her illicit sex acts. There was a clear implication that she would testify to anything the D.A. wanted in return for a promise of leniency.

The same applied to Peggy Satterlee. She had confessed in court that she had submitted to an illegal abortion [it had no relation to the Flynn case].

Peggy took the witness stand looking like a very young girl. She was wearing a demure dress with a Peter Pan collar, bobby sox, and flat-heeled shoes. She looked like everybody's kid sister, instead of the nightclub dancer she really was.

When Giesler began his cross-examination of her, he held a photograph in his hand.

"Miss Satterlee," he said, "I am a little bit mystified. I have here a picture. Is that you?"

He handed her the picture. She looked at it and handed it back.

"Yes," she said.

"Tsk, tsk," he said mildly. But he made no move to show the picture to the judge, the jury, or anyone else—in fact, he never did show them the picture. "What a difference! Tell me, do you always dress like this?"

"Like what?" she demanded.

"In bobby sox and pigtails?"

"Sometimes, if I feel like it."

"That's all," he said.

The jury clearly got the point.

During the trial, an anonymous tipster on the telephone told Giesler that an attendant in a certain funeral parlor could give him some interesting information about Peggy Satterlee. At the funeral parlor Giesler learned that Peggy had visited the mortuary with a boyfriend, Owen Cathcart-Jones, a flier. She had danced about the cold room, pulling up the sheets and peering under them at the nude bodies.

But how could Giesler get this information, which would bear heavily on Peggy's sexual peculiarities and her credibility as a witness, before the jury? He could not call Cathcart-

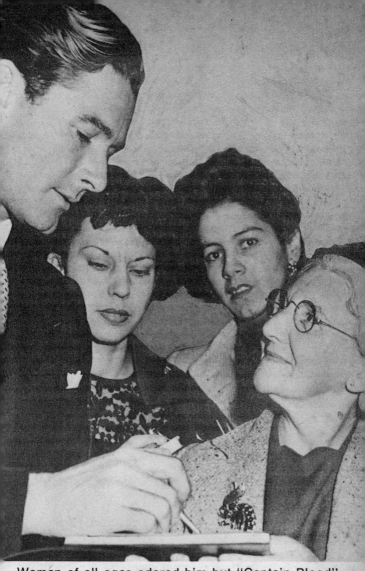

Women of all ages adored him but "Captain Blood" liked them young. By the time Betty Hansen said he took her to bed with his shoes on, "In like Flynn" was standard English. *Los Angeles Times Photo*

Jones. Somehow he had to induce the prosecution to put the flier on the stand.

So the wily Giesler kept throwing the name of the flier into the cross-examination, as though there was some mysterious connection between Peggy and Cathcart-Jones. This led to one of the most hilarious bits of unintentional courtroom humor, when Giesler asked Peggy if the flier had any pet names for her.

A. Rather silly names, but Scrumpet, Bitchy Pie, and so forth.

Q. Scrumpet, Bitchy Pie, and so forth?

A. Scrumpet.

Q. Did you say scrumpet or strumpet?

A. Scrumpet or something. It is an English name for crumpet or . . .

Q. Well?

A. I know it was something.

Q. You know it sounded something like Scrumpet?

A. Yes, sir.

THE JUDGE: I understood her to say Strumpet.

COCHRAN: No, it is a little cake, I think.

The prosecutor thought he saw through Giesler's plan. So he decided he wouldn't let the jurors get the idea that there was anything sinister between Cathcart-Jones and Peggy. He called Cathcart-Jones as a witness.

And Giesler pounced.

On the cross-examination, Giesler asked Cathcart-Jones about the funeral home.

Q. You also were with her down to a mortuary down here in Los Angeles, were you not?

A. Yes.

Q. And she was kind of playing hide-and-seek around the corpses, wasn't she? Do you remember that night?

A. Yes.

Q. Do you remember she showed you—opened it up and showed you—the body of an elderly lady?

A. Yes.

Q. And pulled the sheet down in the mortuary on a Filipino who had been crippled across his center?

A. Yes, I remember that.

Q. And then went back to where they inject the veins of corpses and there opened and looked down at an elderly man

Peggy *(hand at cheek)* and Flynn as they listened to evidence. Attorney Geisler, who diverted the jury's attention from Flynn to the girls, changed the name of the game in rape trials.   *Los Angeles Times Photo*

lying there, and her head was pushed down against the man's face. Do you remember that?

A. Yes, I remember that.

That gamy testimony really shook the jury, which was composed of nine women and three men.

Peggy was utterly destroyed by Giesler's defense witnesses, a harbormaster and two sea captains, who demonstrated that Peggy could not have seen the moon when and where she said she did. It was on the other side of the yacht.

Flynn acquitted himself well on the witness stand, denying everything in a persuasive, believable manner, answering all questions in a crisp, straightforward manner.

Once in a while the famous Flynn sense of humor showed through briefly. There was the time when Cochran recalled to Flynn the testimony of Peggy that she had drunk some milk with rum in it. Flynn said he didn't remember her drinking the concoction. "It just strikes me as a very peculiar thing to drink," he said blandly.

In his charge, the judge told the jurors, "You are not required to believe anything as jurors that you would not believe in the ordinary walk of life."

The jurors decided they did not believe the girls. After deliberating for four hours, they acquitted Flynn on all counts.

Errol Flynn made many movies after that. The scandal didn't affect his popularity in the least.

Gradually, however, he began to show the effects of age and dissipation, and the bad times that fell upon Hollywood with the advent of television eventually left him without movie roles. He appeared in some foreign films to make enough money for his ex-wives, wrote one of the best Hollywood autobiographies ever published, *My Wicked, Wicked Ways,* and got mixed up in a comic opera sort of way with Fidel Castro's very real revolution in Cuba.

He dedicated the book "to a small companion," who was Beverly Aadland. She had been fifteen and a virgin, according to her complacent mother, when he first acquired her as his child love. Obviously, the statutory rape trial had taught Flynn nothing in the way of discretion.

In October 1959 Flynn flew with Beverly to Vancouver, where he was making arrangements to sell his yacht—not the *Sirocco,* but its successor, the *Zaca.* At the airport Flynn told the Canadian reporters, "The rest of my life will be devoted to women and litigation."

When Beverly Aadland appeared with him in *Cuban Rebel Girls,* Flynn winked about his latest teen-age love and said, "The rest of my life will be devoted to women and litigation."

Looking at Beverly, he winked and said, "I like young women because they give you a feeling of youth."

A few days later he prepared to leave Vancouver. Before he left, a small, informal party was held for him. He was in high spirits, joking, telling wonderful, wild stories of Hollywood in its heyday, being the life of the party.

Suddenly, he asked his host, Dr. Grant Gould, if he might lie down for a moment in another room. "I feel sort of tired," Flynn said.

In a few moments, Flynn was dead.

Chaplin's child bride and co-star, Lita Grey, told the court he was "degenerate." Lita's mother and an ill-timed pregnancy converted Chaplin's troubles from statutory rape to a shotgun wedding.

The Museum of Modern Art / Film Stills Archive

8 Charlie Chaplin:
Blood Won't Tell

Charles Chaplin lived through almost all of Hollywood's scandals, so he should have learned prudence. Fatty Arbuckle was his friend. So was Edna Purviance, who figured in the William Desmond Taylor murder mystery. And Wallace Reid. And many, many others.

But Chaplin apparently didn't learn a thing from the troubles of others. He didn't even learn from his own narrow escapes.

In 1918 he began squiring Mildred Harris around Hollywood. The trouble with that romance was that Mildred, a blue-eyed, shapely blonde, was only sixteen. But before he could get into legal difficulties because of her age, Chaplin married her. In 1920 Mildred divorced him.

In 1924 another young cutie came along. She was Lita Grey. She was only sixteen, too. She quickly became his "protégée," inherited Miss Purviance's dressing room (Edna had once been Charlie's great passion, too), and was signed as the star of *The Gold Rush* at seventy-five dollars a week. Charlie was a fool when it came to women, but not about money.

Eight months later, Chaplin had a visit from Lita's uncle, who happened to be an attorney. He pointed out to Charlie that she was below the age of consent, which meant that intimacies with her constituted statutory rape. Charlie got the point. On November 24, 1924 Charlie and Lita, flanked by their respective lawyers, were married in the dreary railroad town of Empalme, near Guaymas, Mexico. That afternoon the glum-faced groom went fishing—alone. When they got back to Hollywood, Charlie made another woman the star of *The Gold Rush.*

Lita and Charlie didn't hit it off together. After they finally broke up, she filed a forty-two page divorce complaint against him on January 10, 1927. In it she charged that Chaplin had been intimate with her for several months before their marriage (while she was still underage), that he had abnormal urges, that he had been mentally cruel to her, even to the extent of suggesting that she commit suicide, and that he was in love with another woman.

At once the guardians of the nation's morals hit the trail in full cry. And Chaplin gave them a legal basis for their hurrahing when he is alleged to have told reporters, "I married Lita Grey because I loved her and, like many other fool men, I loved her more when she wronged me and I am afraid I still love her. I was stunned and ready for suicide that day when she told me she didn't love me but that we must marry. Lita's mother often suggested to me that I marry Lita and I said I would love to if only we could have children. I thought I was incapable of fatherhood. Her mother deliberately and continuously put Lita in my path. She encouraged our relations."

That seemed a pretty clear-cut admission of premarital relations which could land Charlie in prison and on a boycott list. But the candor of his statement swayed many moviegoers. And the United States of 1927 was a good deal more sophisticated than the United States of 1922. By that time it was obvious that relaxed standards were not unique to Hollywood, that every small town and big city in the country had been affected by the changes sweeping the country.

Charlie was able to ride out the storm. He was not prosecuted for whatever may have transpired between him and Lita before their marriage. His career remained intact.

But millions of Americans tucked the memory of that scandal away in the back of their minds. It would be brought forth again when a new and far worse scandal broke on Chaplin's head seventeen years later.

Charles Chaplin was born into dire poverty in London's Limehouse District on April 16, 1889. His parents were small-time vaudeville entertainers. His father died of alcoholism when Charlie was three. The mother, Hannah, made a valiant effort to care for Charlie and his brother, Sydney, who was four years older than he. She quit the theater and took sewing jobs to eke out a bare living for the family. But it wasn't enough: hunger was a familiar thing to them, and it was always hard to scrape up money for the rent on the bare little place in Kensington.

The struggle was too much for Mrs. Chaplin. She had a mental breakdown that put her into a hospital. The two small boys slept in parks, ate scraps, roamed the streets until finally they were caught and sent to a workhouse orphanage, as bad as anything in Dickens' novels.

Then the mother recovered, temporarily, at least. Charlie sold newspapers, barefooted, because shoes were more than he could afford. He opened carriage doors for a penny tip, ran errands, was lather boy in a barber shop.

He had discovered talents within himself. He could mimic, sing, dance, and clown in droll fashion. Soon there were small engagements in the English music halls. Then he became part of a big-time act, Karno's Comedians, which even had bookings in America.

It was in New York that Mack Sennett spotted him, lured him away from Karno's troupe to do just one film, and found he had a comic genius on his hands. Chaplin's starting salary in motion pictures was $150 a week; the first time he got an increase, they raised his salary to $1,250 a week.

Chaplin went on to become the greatest name in the American film art. His character, The Little Fellow, or the tramp, as most moviegoers thought of him, was enormously popular with audiences around the world, and yet philosophers and psychologists found endless subtle meaning in it. His great silent comedies are unequaled.

But with *The Great Dictator* Chaplin proved that he could do as well with sound. Indeed, he even composed the music for all his films, in addition to writing them, producing them, and directing them.

He became one of the richest men in Hollywood; at the

same time, he acquired the reputation of being a tight man with a dollar. He never took out American citizenship, for reasons that have never been quite clear. But he did feel free to participate, in the manner of a dilettante, in politics, at least to the extent of endorsing Communist-front organizations. He had been sympathetic to radical causes, and to the Soviet Union, as long ago as the early 1920s, probably as a result of his bitter childhood experiences. Anti-Communists were hostile to him, the strongly nationalistic sentiments generated by World War II made his failure to become an American a suspect thing, and his wealth didn't endear him to most people.

In his pictures, Chaplin liked to give the lead to an unknown, whom he would build up as a star. Often, the star's career was short-lived, as with Myrna Kennedy, a girl barely out of school who was chosen for the feminine lead in *The Circus,* was lionized for one season, and then fell back into obscurity. Nobody to Celebrity to Nobody again: that seemed to be the pattern.

It was different with Paulette Goddard. Chaplin built her into a star and trained her, but she remained with him for years. He steadfastly refused to say whether they were married, although she lived with him in his house openly. Actually, they had been married on a ship at Canton, China, in 1936, but he thought that his marital affairs were nobody's business but his own. Most people, of course, assumed the worst, and this did not add to Chaplin's personal popularity nor to his reputation for morality.

In 1941, Paulette Goddard and Chaplin separated. She later got a Mexican divorce.

A bachelor again, Chaplin began having Sunday afternoon tea-and-crumpets parties in his big, baroque mansion on Summit Drive above Beverly Hills. At those gatherings one might meet Greta Garbo, John Garfield, John McCormack, David Niven, Katharine Hepburn, Ronald Colman, Errol Flynn, Gary Cooper. People felt quite free to bring guests, and to ask if friends might go to a Sunday afternoon at Chaplin's. In 1941, A. C. Blumenthal, the producer, sent a girl to Tim Durant, a Chaplin associate, with a letter of introduction explaining that he had met her in Mexico City.

The girl that Durant saw was a twenty-year-old redhead from Brooklyn who had been trying to break into movies for two years, although he was unaware of that fact. To him she

Chaplin strolling with Paulette Goddard in Pebble Beach. They lived together for years, insisting it was nobody's business if they were married. (They were.)

Freda Keefer Collection

looked like a pretty Irish stenographer. She was very demure when he saw her with her mother. And so he invited her to come out to Chaplin's house any Sunday afternoon for tea, crumpets, and good conversation.

The girl's name was Joan Barry. Chaplin paid off for years for the trouble he got into because of her.

In 1942, Joan Barry walked into movie columnist Hedda Hopper's office. She said she was desperate. She said she thought she was pregnant; she was at the end of her rope. The columnist took her to a doctor who confirmed the diagnosis. Joan said that the father was Chaplin.

In the weeks that followed, she tried to force her way into Chaplin's house on several occasions. When she realized that he was determined not to see her, she took an overdose of sleeping pills. The cops found her in time, pumped out her stomach, and booked her as a vagrant. Judge Charles J. Griffin, sitting in Beverly Hills Police Court, suspended sentence on condition that she leave town at once and for good. Chaplin gave a friend, Robert Arden, money to give Joan a ticket to New York and one hundred dollars. This was an act of generosity which was to boomerang. Police Captain W. W. White escorted Joan to the train.

Joan didn't go to New York. She got as far as Omaha, then left the train and caught the next one back to Los Angeles. She broke into Chaplin's home and, in desperation, he called the police. The judge gave her a ninety-day sentence. Chaplin sent his attorney to intercede for her. After she had spent five days in jail, he got her out of there and into a hospital in Santa Monica.

Chaplin's butler, who disliked his boss—and subsequently testified against him—put in a discreet telephone call to Hedda Hopper. She got hold of her sidekick, Florabel Muir, Hollywood correspondent of the *New York Daily News* (which syndicated Miss Hopper's column), and the two succeeded in what Miss Hopper has called their "attempt at kidnapping." They hid Joan in Florabel Muir's own house.

And then Joan Barry began to tell her story to the newspaper women—and the world.

She said she was pregnant. She said Charles Chaplin was the father.

She slapped him with a paternity suit. Pending trial of the case, he was ordered to pay one hundred dollars a week support, plus twenty-five hundred dollars immediately for her care, plus forty-six hundred dollars in installments for medical expenses.

A federal grand jury, intrigued by the newspaper accounts, summoned Joan Barry for questioning. It returned two indictments. One charged Charlie Chaplin with violation of the Mann Act, which outlaws the interstate transportation of women for immoral purposes. The other indictment accused him of having violated Joan's civil rights.

The Mann Act indictment was based on a trip that Joan had made to New York in the fall of 1942. Two weeks later Chaplin had gone to New York, too, to make a speech supporting a second front in Europe. They did not stay in the same hotel in New York, but Joan Barry said that one night she had gone with him to his suite in the Waldorf Towers, where they engaged in sexual intercourse. After they returned separately to Los Angeles, Chaplin again had relations with her, she said.

The civil rights indictment grew out of Joan's arrest—the arrest which ended with her being given one hundred dollars and a one-way ticket to New York. Indicted with Chaplin were the judge, Griffin; the police captain, White; Chaplin's friend, Arden; his associate, Durant; Police Lieutenant Claude Marple; and Police Matron Jessie Billie Reno. The penalty for this offense was a maximum of two years' imprisonment, a ten-thousand-dollar fine, or both. As it turned out, this indictment was eventually dropped.

But Chaplin was brought to trial on the Mann Act charge. Like Errol Flynn, he got Jerry Giesler to defend him.

There were seven women on the jury that tried Chaplin. The federal judge was J. F. T. O'Connor. The prosecutor was United States Attorney Charles H. Carr.

On the eve of the trial, the *Los Angeles Times* outlined what Giesler's line of defense would be. It was an accurate report. The paper even put it in the kind of words that Giesler might use:

"Ladies and gentlemen of the jury, at this time it is my duty to outline my defendant's case. We hope to establish to your satisfaction that he is innocent of violating the Mann Act as set forth in regard to the young lady, Joan Barry. She came to Los Angeles in 1941, met Chaplin and began to go out socially. We will show that he interested her in pictures, that he believed a screen career was possible for her, and that following up that belief, he arranged a contract for her. Thereafter he provided for her dramatic lessons with Max Reinhardt. He also instructed her himself. We will show that her teeth were fixed at the expense of Chaplin Studios, that he bought a story for her, the purchase price of which was fifteen thousand dollars. Further, she received a bonus of one thousand dollars. In September 1942, she was irked at the long delay in preparing her story for the screen and told Chaplin that she wanted to go to New York with her mother to live. Chaplin said, 'I have a lot of money invested in you.' She said, 'I am going anyway.' Mr. Chaplin said, 'All right, go. Arrangements will be made for your tickets.' It was all open and aboveboard. The canceled checks which paid for her tickets can be produced.

"We will show that prior to October 1, 1942, she and her mother were occupying the same apartment in Beverly Hills and that she gave up the apartment and went to visit her aunt in New York City. She arrived there on October 5, moved into the Waldorf-Astoria, checking out of there on October 10. Mr. Chaplin did not arrive until October 15. Miss Barry checked in at another New York hotel which was owned by a man she had seen in Mexico. She stayed there from October 10 until October 25. During that time she went out with the person who had checked her in. This person took her to the Stork Club. Mr. Chaplin happened to be there and saw her dancing with another man, but the two parties did not join.

"The sole occasion when she saw Mr. Chaplin in New York was the night at the Stork Club. On that occasion she did accompany him to the Waldorf hotel but Mr. Chaplin will deny that there was any intimacy. We will show that she was willingly and gratuitously available to him to have relations at any time before her trip to New York, but at no time which involves the Mann Act charge against my client.

"Mr. Chaplin stayed in New York until October 27 and did not see Miss Barry again. He did not pay her bills at her other hotel nor did the Chaplin Studios.

"Briefly, it is the position of this defendant that he did not transport Joan Barry to New York for the purpose of having intimate relations. Nor did he insist upon her returning to Los Angeles for purposes of intimacy.''

Key testimony, of course, was that of the alleged "victim" herself. She admitted that she had had two abortions before her present pregnancy.

She was asked if it wasn't true that on two occasions she had threatened to "put his name in the headlines" and to "make trouble for him"—threats that had amounted to black-mail. She denied it.

She did concede, however, that she had broken into Chap-lin's house, had pointed a loaded gun at Chaplin for an hour and a half, had then gone to bed with him for sexual inter-course.

(Giesler later commented that he couldn't imagine anyone believing that Chaplin would send Joan to New York, keep her there in an expensive hotel suite, and pay her fare back to Los Angeles for immoral purposes when he could have her any time he wanted "for as little as twenty-five cents carfare.")

A writer was called as a witness, and he admitted that he'd gone out with Joan a good deal and that she'd visited him in his apartment.

Another very reluctant witness was Jean Paul Getty, the oil billionaire. Giesler had referred repeatedly to a Tulsa oil mogul who had befriended Joan. Finally he called Getty to the stand.

Under Giesler's questioning, Getty conceded that he was acquainted with Joan.

"Early in 1941 did you see her frequently?" Giesler asked.

"Yes," Getty replied, after the judge overruled an objection by the prosecutor.

"Did you see her in Mexico City in March 1941?"

This time the judge sustained the prosecutor's objection.

"Did you see her in Tulsa in November 1942?"

"Yes."

"Did you see her in Brownsville, Texas—" Giesler began, but he was interrupted by objections and had to drop that line of questioning.

In that trial and in the paternity trial that followed, however, Giesler was able to establish as a matter of record that Getty had been footing the bill for a good many of Joan's expenses, especially for items like railroad tickets and hotel rooms.

Giesler's point was that Joan had been traveling about, not to provide boudoir entertainment for Chaplin, but for the benefit of "a man she had been keeping company with and who took her to Mexico." In New York, said Giesler, the girl registered at the fashionable Hotel Pierre "through the connivance of this man who owns the hotel." Getty owned the Pierre.

There were other implications, to which Getty replied out of

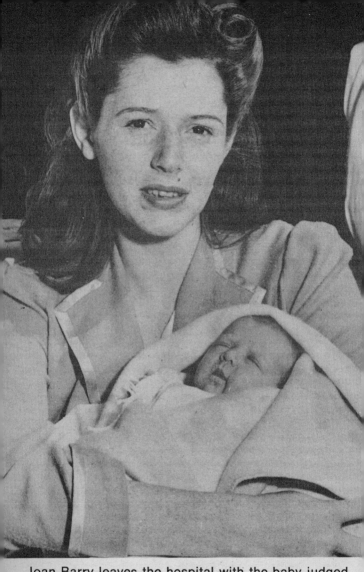

Joan Barry leaves the hospital with the baby judged in a paternity suit to be Chaplin's child, despite blood tests to the contrary. Jean Paul Getty was a reluctant witness at the trial. *Wide World Photos*

court by saying, "It's ridiculous for Giesler to insinuate that Joan tried to blackmail me and that I had to give her money under threat. She never at any time in the years I have known her made any unpleasant threats of any kind."

Chaplin took the stand in his own behalf. He showed himself, in Giesler's opinion, to be "the best witness I've ever seen in a law court." He managed to look humble, whether he felt that way or not. He also gave the impression of candor.

"Yes, I was intimate with her," he said, weeping. "I liked the girl."

After five hours of deliberation, the jury acquitted Chaplin of a charge which could have resulted in twenty-five years in prison and a twenty-five-thousand-dollar fine.

It looked like Chaplin's troubles were over. They weren't.

Before the paternity suit came to trial, Joan had her baby, whom she named Carol Ann. Three eminent pathologists—Drs. Roy W. Hammack, Newton Evans, and Vernon L. Andrews—made tests of the blood of Joan, Charlie, and the baby. It was their unanimous opinion that Chaplin could not possibly be the baby's father; it was a scientific impossibility.

Nevertheless, Joan's new lawyer, Joseph Scott, opposed a motion by Chaplin to have the paternity suit thrown out of court. Superior Court Judge Stanley Mosk agreed that "the ends of justice will best be served by a full and fair trial of the issues."

It seemed apparent that the trial would only be a formality, however. So Chaplin dropped Giesler and put his defense in the hands of his then regular attorney.

Scott's great emotional appeal wound up with these ringing words to the jury: "There has been no one to stop Chaplin in his lecherous conduct all these years—except you. Wives and mothers all over the country·are watching to see you stop him dead in his tracks. You'll sleep well the night you give this baby a name—the night you show him the law means him as well as the bums on Skid Row."

It wasn't good enough to win for Joan, but it was good enough to prevent a verdict in favor of Chaplin in the face of the scientific evidence exonerating him.

At a second trial Chaplin was adjudged the father of the child. The baby was allotted support of seventy-five dollars a week, to be increased to one hundred in time. And the child was entitled to the name of Chaplin.

Chaplin was understandably bitter about the verdict. He

must have regretted the words he spoke after his acquittal on the Mann Act charge: "I've always had an abiding faith in the American people and justice."

But in the second paternity trial, as Dr. Vladimir Eliasberg wrote in the *Southern California Law Review* of July 1946, "The Chaplin jury let sentimental considerations turn logic out of doors and failed dismally in its task of weighing the evidence."

In 1953 the California legislature passed a law outlawing paternity trials after blood tests have proved that the defendant cannot be the father.

While the trials were pending, the fifty-four-year-old comedian contracted his fourth marriage, to eighteen-year-old Oona O'Neill. It was to be his happiest marital venture.

It was the only happy thing in Chaplin's life for many years to follow. After the war, as the Cold War got under way, Chaplin's support of left-wing causes brought him under fire more and more. People began to be reluctant to be seen with him, to associate with him. One of his greatest movies, *Monsieur Verdoux,* was picketed and boycotted so effectively that it had to be withdrawn from exhibition.

In 1952, after *Limelight* was previewed for Hollywood's elite—it earned their unanimous praise—Chaplin and his young bride took their children, who then numbered four, for a vacation in Europe. Their ship was no sooner at sea than the Attorney General, James P. McGranery, announced that he was rescinding Chaplin's reentry permit. Chaplin couldn't return without a hearing. He could be held in custody as long as two years if he tried to come back.

Embittered still more—feeling, with reason, that the American authorities had resorted to cheap trickery to hit him instead of granting him an open hearing while he was in the United States—Chaplin decided against returning to Hollywood. He and Oona, with their numerous offspring, settled at Vevey, near Lausanne, in Switzerland. In the 1970s, Chaplin was knighted by Queen Elizabeth II.

In 1953 Joan was found wandering barefoot, in a daze, on the streets of Torrance, California. She had arrived there from Mexico City, as nearly as the police could make out from her jumbled comments. She was taken to the psychopathic ward of Harbor General Hospital and then released. A few hours later she was again found wandering in a state of mental imbalance. Returned to the hospital, she was examined by a

Hedda Hopper, who conducted a one-woman campaign against "dubious relationships" in general and Charlie in particular. She hated both his love life and his politics.   *The Museum of Modern Art/Film Stills Archive*

staff psychiatrist, Dr. V. J. Miller, who described her as a schizophrenic with a well-organized delusional pattern. She was living in a world of fantasy. Judge William P. Haughton, sitting in Superior Court, committed Joan to a state hospital.

The big Chaplin mansion that witnessed such stormy scenes has been destroyed. The estate was subdivided. Now a covey of modern houses cover the site.

9 Lupe Velez:
She Didn't Believe in Marriage

"I am no hypocrite," Lupe Velez used to say, and everyone agreed with her. It was the custom for some Hollywood correspondents to write her name: "Lupe (rhymes with Whoopee!)" In a free-wheeling movie capital, she was the least inhibited of stars. Her customary greeting was a kiss instead of a handshake. At parties she occasionally climaxed her boasts about her charms by lifting her dress up about her neck; since she usually wore nothing under her dress, this was fairly effective proof of her claims.

She was only five feet one and a half inches tall and weighed a mere one hundred and twelve pounds. She looked like a teenager, and in fact she was only eighteen when she became a star. That may have been her curse, for throughout the rest of her life she was known for her adolescent appetites, her childish whims, the gaiety and the rage that seemed as shallow and brief as a bobbysoxer's.

But all this makes her sound unattractive and nothing could be farther from the truth. Everybody loved Lupe. She was warm-hearted, generous, kind, fun-loving, and utterly without

Gary Cooper and Lupe ("Rhymes with Whoopee") in a scene from *Wolf Song*. He couldn't keep up with her demands. *The Museum of Modern Art/Film Stills Archive*

malice. In short, she had not only the faults of a teenager, but the virtues of one, too.

Born in San Luis Potosi, Mexico, on July 10, 1908, she was christened Guadalupe Velez de Villalobos. Her convent schooling ended when she was fourteen, and she went to work as a shopgirl in Mexico City. She studied dancing and appeared as the lead in a musical comedy staged by the dancing school. A producer decided she had the making of a dramatic actress and gave her a part in a Mexico City production of *Rataplan.* The American actor, Richard Bennett, visiting the Mexican capital, told her he thought she'd do well in motion pictures. Her first film job was in a Hal Roach comedy. In a very short time she won the feminine lead opposite Douglas Fairbanks in United Artists' *The Gaucho,* filmed in 1927 and released in 1928. For the next seventeen years she was one of the major names in Hollywood.

Her first love affair, as everyone knew—for Lupe was nothing if not indiscreet—was with Jack Gilbert. Hedda Hopper, in her memoirs, *From Under My Hat,* recalls Lupe asking her, about that time, whether she should marry Gilbert. "After all," Lupe pointed out, "I'm no lady."

Miss Hopper replied with a question of her own: "Lupe, what's the advantage of getting married? Tell me now, honestly."

Lupe took that as the answer she'd been waiting for. Beaming happily, she dashed to Gilbert's bungalow, yelling, "Hey, Jack, we don't have to get married. . . ."

Gary Cooper was the most famous of Lupe's lovers. They met while acting together in the 1929 Western, *Wolf Song.* In later years Cooper would display the demeanor of a deacon—although a woman like Anita Ekberg was still capable of having a rousing effect on him—but in those days, when Cooper had just graduated from extra to star, he was one of the livelier spirits in Hollywood.

He bought Lupe an eagle for a pet. But she was too enthusiastic about sex to think that any creature should be forced to live without it. So he personally went out and trapped another eagle to keep it company. (The second eagle turned out to be a male, like the first.)

Lupe's antics—the time a horse nipped her and she turned around and bit the horse, for example—appeared endlessly amusing to Cooper. But the time came when he found her too demanding, too possessive, too exhausting.

Then Johnny Weissmuller, screen Tarzan, came along in 1933. He became Lupe's only husband. The marriage was a wild, violent succession of separations, reconciliations, and rows, ending finally in divorce in 1938.

After that the men came more frequently and lasted only briefly. The best known was Arturo de Cordova. Most of the others were undistinguished movie hopefuls and fringe characters. Often Lupe would show up in a nightclub with six or seven men in tow, and it was difficult to tell which of them was The Man. Perhaps they all were.

Lupe was famous for her dogs, a Sealyham and a Scottish terrier, Chips and Chops; for the pair of seats reserved for her for nearly two decades at a prize fight arena; for her extravagantly decorated house, in which her bedroom, furnished with a bar, was the center of activity. The bedroom was thirty feet long. It was all white—walls, ceiling, carpet, draperies, bed covers. The bed was eight feet square.

"We got so many people goin' in and out of this house—thirty a day, I'll bet—we can't keep in cigarettes," Lupe once said. She said she didn't give parties every day, "they just stop in—I come home sometimes and I say, 'Is this where I live?' But I love it. If I can't live this way I don' wanna live at all."

In the latter part of the Thirties, there were signs that Lupe's career was nearing an end. She did a number of *Mexican Spitfire* comedies, but little else, and soon they stopped, too. In 1938 she was on Broadway with Libby Holman and Clifton Webb in *You Never Know.* Then she made a couple of Mexican movies, *Nana* and *Zaza.*

"Why should I worry?" she said in 1944. I know I'm not worth anything, I can't sing well, I can't dance well. I've never done a thing that I like . . . and it comes from the bottom of my heart or I wouldn't say it."

Asked her ambition, she said, "I just want to have a little fun."

Fun, to Lupe, usually meant a man. Or men. She didn't believe in loving "just one man," as she often said. "There is no such thing as love the way we speak of it," she said. "There is just possession, that's what we humans have done to love. If you love a man you're supposed to sit home, sad and blue, waiting till he gets there. You go out with another man to have a good time, he gets mad—that's possession. And they ain't gonna possess me because I'm not sad and blue for anybody. I've got so many friends."

Johnny Weissmuller, her only legal mate, was more than a match for the Mexican Spitfire. She would flash her bare bottom at parties, and when he got mad he threw food at her. That's not Lupe he's carrying here.

The Museum of Modern Art/Film Stills Archive

When Lupe's career was on the skids, even the Mexican Spitfire comedies stopped. "Why should I worry?" said Lupe. "I just want to have a little fun."

The police who found Lupe's body said, "She looked so small in that outsize bed that we thought at first she was a doll." *Copyright, 1942 RKO Radio Pictures, Inc.*

But Lupe Velez was just putting on a brave front. The teenager who never grew up knew at that moment that life was closing in on her. Life was closing in—and so was death.

His name was Harold Maresch, but he used the name "Harald Ramond" in his attempts to break into the movies. He was born in Austria of a French opera singer and a Yugoslav business man. At least that's what he always said. He was young and darkly handsome, and he told wonderful stories about his past, which was, as he told it, very adventurous— fighting the Nazis in Vienna and Prague, being captured and sent to Dachau concentration camp, escaping from Dachau and making his way to France, fighting the Nazis in Paris, then fleeing to the U.S. In wartime Hollywood, it sounded terribly romantic and exciting.

It was not surprising that Lupe should conceive a passion for the twenty-seven-year-old actor. And it must have been at least flattering to him, as well as convenient. She took him everywhere and introduced him to everyone. Doors opened that might otherwise have been closed. But it was, like all of Lupe's "romances," a tempestuous affair. After a time, she began to have mixed feelings about the relationship.

About the beginning of November 1944, Lupe gave Mary Morris of the New York newspaper *PM*, now defunct, an interview which was far more significant than most of the people who read it—or even Miss Morris herself—realized. Lupe told her she'd been in love. The reporter said that was nice.

"*No*, darling," Lupe said, "I was like a fool with a very unworthy person. Nobody saw me for years; I buried myself for this man so he could shine."

The question of marriage arose. This is how Mary Morris reported Lupe's reaction:

"Lupe finally turned her head from the mirror, gazed at me for several seconds, then, with her voice pitched very low, for emphasis, she said, 'I don't believe in marriage, darling.' "

"She paused for this to make its total effect, then she continued. 'If there's children, okay. But a woman who has a career; today we're here, tomorrow we're sent somewhere. We travel; in our work we have lots of men friends. . . . I'm practical: husband and career don't mix.' "

A few days later Lupe went to a doctor's office. When she left his office, she was biting her lip to keep back tears. She went to her home, where a birthday party was being held for her brother-in-law.

Lupe drew her sister into her bedroom and closed the door. "Darling," she began, "I need help."

"Lupe, I'd do anything for you," she told her.

Lupe began to sob. She told her sister that she was going to have a baby. She was more than three months' pregnant.

"We made plans," her sister said later. "Lupe begged me to leave with her and go to Mexico. She said, 'You are married and can take the baby. Josie, I need your company so bad. We will go away.' "

"I said to her, 'Of course, Lupe, if you need me I will go, but first I want to go back with my husband to San Antonio and see about a house we are planning there.' "

"She cried again and begged me to write soon. Then she said, 'Josie, you come right back and we will have another long talk and then go away.' "

Lupe told her business manager, Bo Roos, that she was pregnant. "I asked Ramond what he intended to do about it," Roos said. "He said he would have to have a little time to think it over. Then he proposed a mock ceremony." Finally Harald said he'd marry Lupe only if she'd sign a document saying that she knew he was marrying her only to give her baby a name.

Her reply to that was a telephone call to Louella O. Parsons, the Hollywood columnist who had publicly announced the Velez-Ramond engagement the previous July. The breakup of the couple had not been announced. So Lupe called Lolly to tell her, "We had one big battle and I told him to get out of my house." When Lolly asked Lupe how Ramond spelled his name, the actress replied, "I don't know. I never did know. Who cares?"

And then she added, "I like my dogs, Chips and Chops, better." Which was undoubtedly true.

Still the fact of Lupe's pregnancy was a secret. But it was a fact that had to be dealt with, and quickly. Lupe called Roos.

"Well, so," she said. "It looks like I either have to go to Mexico for a while or to a doctor. What do you think?"

That night Lupe went to a premiere of her latest Mexican film, *Zaza,* with two friends, Estelle Taylor, former wife of Jack Dempsey, and Benita Oakie, wife of screen star Jack Oakie. Afterwards they all went back to Lupe's house.

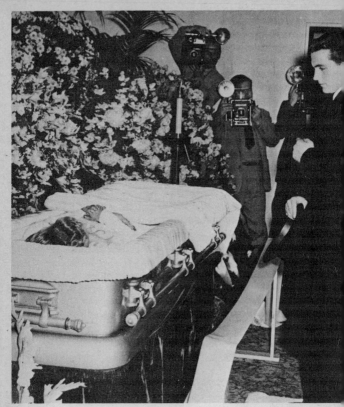

Asked how Harald Ramond spelled his name, Lupe replied, "I don't know. I never did know. Who cares?" He felt equal indifference to her pregnancy, but he did show up for the funeral. *Los Angeles Times Photo*

Roos called her there about 10:30 p.m. During their telephone conversation earlier in the day she had talked of suicide, and he had been worrying about it all day. He pleaded with her now not to kill herself. "Her last words," he recalled, "were a promise that she would do nothing until I talked to her the next day."

For hours Lupe talked with her two women friends about her predicament.

"I'm just weary with the whole world," she said. "People think that I fight. I have to fight for everything. I'm so tired of it all. Ever since I was a baby, I've been fighting. I've never met a man with whom I didn't have to fight to exist."

Miss Taylor said Lupe talked constantly of the baby.

"She said she had plenty of time to get rid of it," Miss Taylor recalled, "but she said, 'It's my baby, I couldn't commit murder and still live myself. I would rather kill myself.'"

In those hours of anguished conversation, it became apparent that Lupe Velez, the uninhibited, had always wanted a baby. That she hungered just as painfully for the respectability and security of married life. Many women have borne children out of wedlock and reared them themselves, or arranged for their care, but Lupe Velez would be content with nothing less than a proper, respectable marriage.

Finally the other women had to leave. It was then 3:20 a.m. Miss Taylor said she was afraid to go to her car alone. Lupe went with her.

"I don't know what you could be afraid of," Lupe said. "I'm getting to the place where the only thing of which I'm afraid is life itself."

The car went down the drive and away from the big Spanish-style house on North Rodeo Drive. The little figure in the driveway stood looking after it until the red taillights could no longer be seen. It was very still. Silence lay like a mantle over the quiet streets.

Lupe went back to her bedroom. She lay on the bed, thinking—if the chaos in her hurt mind could be called thinking. About dawn she wrote two notes in her own eccentric English.

One note said:

"To Harald:

"May God forgive you and forgive me, too, but I prefer to take my life away and our baby's before I bring him with shame or killin [sic] him.

Lupe."

On the back, as an afterthought, she added:

"How could you, Harald, fake such a great love for me and our baby when all the time you didn't want us. I see no other way out for me so goodby and good luck to you.

Love,
Lupe."

The other note was addressed to Lupe's secretary. It said:

"You and you alone know the facts and the reason why I am taking my own life. Forgive me and don't think bad of me. I love you, Mammy, so take care of my mother. And so goodby and try to forgive me. Say goodby to all my friends and to the American press that always was so nice to me."

Then she put on blue silk pajamas, brushed her hair carefully, climbed into bed and arranged herself neatly. She picked up a bottle of pills from her bedside table and began swallowing them, washing them down with water from a glass on the table. When she had swallowed them all, she lay back on the pillow.

That was how they found her in the morning, two hours after she died.

The first policeman to arrive at the house said, "She looked so small in that outsize bed that we thought at first she was a doll."

10 Ingrid Bergman:
The Saint Was a Woman

Stromboli is the name of a 3,000-foot volcano in the Lipari Islands, which rise from the Tyrrhenian Sea north of Sicily and west of the toe of Italy. It is also the name of a motion picture directed by Roberto Rossellini in 1949. The filming was done on location on the island of Stromboli. During the production, an eruption occurred. But it was not the volcano.

It was the star, Ingrid Bergman, a cool-looking Swedish beauty who awakened like an Alaskan volcano that has been simmering under a glacier.

In the space of a few months, Ingrid Bergman, who had been admired with something close to adoration by the American moviegoers as a person as ethereal as the St. Joan she had recently portrayed on the screen, was plunged into a scandal of cosmic proportions, even for Hollywood.

Few, if any, of the people who knew her would have expected it, although her friends had known for some time that all was not well with her marriage. In those days Scandinavians were usually thought of as dispassionate folk. That was in the days before the Nordics became famous for films

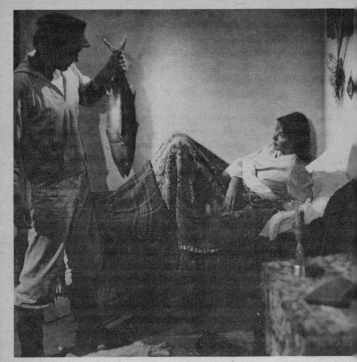

Ingrid Bergman in *Stromboli,* one of six pictures she made with Rossellini. Scenes like this kept America shocked, but the pictures were all duds.

Copyright 1950 RKO Radio Pictures Inc.

like *I Am Curious (Yellow)* and for the broadest public accep-
tance of sexuality in every area of society. This naïve miscon-
ception about Scandinavians prevented most people from
recognizing that Ingrid Bergman was, after all, a woman, with
a richly matured woman's emotions. If anything, the contrast
between American hypocrisy, in the late 1940s, and Swedish
forthrightness about sexual matters probably intensified the
conflicts that developed within her after she came to Hollywood from her native city, Stockholm.

She was born there on August 29, 1915, the only child of Mr.
and Mrs. Justus Bergman. Her father operated a camera
shop. When Ingrid was two, her mother died. Her father's
sister, Ellen, moved into the house and took the place of a
mother.

Her childhood was lonely, in a house with only two elderly
people. As a child, Ingrid was unusually tall, and she was very
self-conscious about her height. She became shy and
avoided other children. She lived in her own little world of
make-believe.

When she was twelve, her father was stricken with an illness
and died. Seven months later, when Ingrid and her Aunt Ellen
were alone together in the house, the aunt died suddenly.
Ingrid went to live with her Uncle Otto and his five children.
For a girl who didn't know how to play with other children, life
with five cousins was agony. And Uncle Otto didn't help,
because he had vehement religious prejudice against the
theater, and he became very angry when he learned that his
young niece had already set her heart on a dramatic career.

Ingrid was sent to a private school for girls. One day the
gymnasium class was canceled and the girls were left in a big
hall, with no teacher and no instructions. So Ingrid went up on
the stage, summoning all her courage, and said, "I will
entertain you." Only a psychiatrist could explain how a child
so frightened of other children could dare such a thing.

The other girls laughed at Ingrid, but she went ahead with
what she had in mind. She told them that she would present a
play and that she would play all the roles herself. She did a
French farce called *The Green Elevator,* which had six parts.

It is a pleasure to record that Ingrid wowed 'em. Their
applause, won the hard way, made that day the happiest in her
life, at least up to that time.

Her two favorite stories were those of Joan of Arc and of
Tristan and Isolde. Joan was courage and human greatness,

Tristan and Isolde was romantic, earthly love, which must have seemed like a remote, unattainable thing for a gawky teenage girl who thought of herself as dreadfully unattractive.

By sheer stubbornness, Ingrid wore down her uncle's resistance. Finally he gave her permission to try for a scholarship to the state-owned Royal Dramatic Theater School after she graduated from high school. He was sure she'd fail the examination.

The test was an audition, held in a playhouse before the judges and the staff instructors. There were more than a hundred candidates that night. After each had completed a reading, there would be polite applause from the judges and instructors. But after Ingrid gave her reading, there wasn't a sound from them. Someone waved his hand as though to say that she could leave the theater, so she went out and trudged unhappily home.

A couple of days later she was notified that she had won a scholarship. Her audience had been too spellbound to applaud.

Never before had Ingrid had a boy friend. But at dramatic school, where she was one of the best students, Ingrid found herself much sought after. Two months after she entered the school she met Peter Lindstrom on a blind date. She was eighteen, he twenty-seven. He was a six-foot-two farm boy who had become a successful dentist in Stockholm.

At the end of her first year in the dramatic school, she was offered a job with Svensk Filmindustrie, one of the biggest Swedish motion picture companies. With the encouragement of Lindstrom, of whom she had been seeing a good deal by then, she decided to go into the movies. In her first film she played the part of a maid in a cheap hotel. Then she played opposite Sweden's matinee idol of the time.

About that time Lindstrom decided he'd rather be a doctor of medicine than a dentist. He began his medical education, but in his spare time he continued to court Ingrid. On July 7, 1936, they became engaged, a few weeks before Ingrid's twenty-first birthday. Almost exactly a year later on July 10, 1937, they were married in the little white Lutheran church at Stode, a lumbering town in northeastern Sweden where Lindstrom's family lived.

Lindstrom, whom Ingrid found to be kind and considerate, had reduced his dental practice to four days a week in order to allow more time for his medical training. In addition, he now took on the active management of Ingrid's business affairs. This was to become a major task, for she was becoming more of a star with each picture.

It must have been difficult for Lindstrom, but he tried manfully to submerge any resentment of her career or any jealousy of the actors with whom she worked. When she made a picture in Berlin for the German company, UFA, Lindstrom stayed in Sweden. But one day she found him waiting for her in the lobby of the Adlon Hotel, where she was staying. He had missed her, so he had come to Berlin. But he had checked in, not at the Adlon, but at a small hotel nearby. He didn't want people to know he was there because he didn't think it was good for an actress to have a husband always hanging around.

On September 20, 1938, a daughter was born to them. They called her Friedel (for Ingrid's mother) Pia (an anagram of the initials of Petter Aron—Lindstrom's middle name—and Ingrid). Three or four months later, Ingrid's last picture before her confinement, *Intermezzo,* was released. David O. Selznick decided to remake the picture in an English-language version and to acquire Miss Bergman as his own star. He sent Katherine (Kay) Brown to her to arrange the deal.

Ingrid was reluctant to leave her husband, who could not spare time from his medical studies, and her baby, who was too young to travel, but Lindstrom insisted that she seize the opportunity. And in her heart Ingrid was eager to do a picture in Hollywood, the movie capital of the world.

So in 1939 she went to Hollywood, alone, to make one picture.

The picture was the remake of *Intermezzo,* with Leslie Howard. When her work on it was done, Ingrid went back to Europe.

Then the war broke out. It seemed likely that Sweden might have to fight. Tension mounted in Stockholm. (Ultimately Sweden's Scandinavian neighbors, Norway, Denmark, and Finland, were drawn into the war, but Sweden itself managed to maintain its neutrality to the end.)

In Hollywood, Selznick released *Intermezzo* to the applause of the critics and the public. He telephoned Ingrid that he was exercising the option in her contract. He wanted her to come back to Hollywood for seven years of picture-making.

Lindstrom, fearful that his wife and baby might be caught up in the war, urged her to accept the offer, even though it would mean a separation for them. He drove Ingrid and Pia, as they always called the baby, across Europe by car to Genoa—Italy was then neutral—where they boarded the *Rex,* the last liner to carry civilian passengers.

When she first arrived in New York, Selznick was unsure of his future production schedule, so she remained in New York long enough to appear on the stage in Ferenc Molnar's *Liliom* with Burgess Meredith.

In May she moved to Hollywood. About the middle of the summer Lindstrom, lonely for his family, came to New York on a Swedish freighter and Ingrid joined him there. He didn't like New York. After two weeks he returned to Sweden.

That September Ingrid made her second Hollywood picture, *Adam Had Four Sons,* on loan to Columbia Pictures. Then she was lent to MGM for *Rage in Heaven,* and after that *Dr. Jekyll and Mr. Hyde.*

Meanwhile Lindstrom had found himself unbearably lonely in Sweden. He asked Ingrid to see if he could get into a medical school in America, so that he could complete his studies closer to her. Through friends of Selznick, she was able to get him into the University of Rochester medical school. They'd be a continent apart, but at least they'd be on the same continent and they could get together from time to time.

In September 1943 he completed his courses at Rochester—and what a chore they must have been, for a professional man learning a new language at the same time!—and transferred to Stanford University in California for postgraduate training. Now he was a mere 480 miles from Ingrid and Pia.

It was probably inevitable that the two should grow apart, for they were really not living together. It was about this time that Ingrid's most intimate friends began to detect the first indications that all was not well with the Lindstrom marriage. She never criticized him to her friends, but they became aware that she herself recognized certain of his shortcomings. (And he undoubtedly was coming to see hers.) Once, when a friend asked her at that time if she'd choose her marriage over her career, she snapped, "Never!"

Nevertheless, in 1944 the Lindstroms bought the first house they'd ever owned, a stone and redwood structure at 1220 North Benedict Canyon Drive. That year they were finally able to live together, as man and wife, in that house, for Lindstrom completed his studies and moved to Los Angeles, where he joined the staff of the County General Hospital.

Gradually the two grew farther and farther apart. His life was in medicine, especially in neurosurgery. He was completely immersed in it. Her life was in the motion picture industry, which gave her an Academy Award for *Gaslight* in 1944 (in 1956 she would win a second Oscar for *Anastasia*). They had different interests, different friends, different activities. He still handled her business affairs, but that didn't help matters, because the executives with whom he had to deal felt that he was high-handed, and her friends thought that he was too domineering in his attitude toward his wife, too.

In the spring of 1946, during a long visit to New York, Ingrid began, for the first time, to be seen in public with men other than her husband, who was back in Los Angeles. Bob Capa, Cary Grant, Whitney Bolton, and others squired her about town. It was undoubtedly all very innocent.

But it showed which way the wind was blowing.

It was during that vacation in New York that she saw *Open City*, one of the greatest films of the immediate postwar period. A semi-documentary written by Federico Fellini and Sergei Amidei, *Open City* was filmed in Italy in 1945. As *The Filmgoer's Companion* puts it, the movie is a "record, shot under the noses of the retreating German army by Italian patriots, of what Italy had suffered under the occupation." (It was also, incidentally, the work which introduced Anna Magnani to the world.)

"Wasn't it wonderful!" Ingrid Bergman exclaimed to her friend and public relations man, Joseph Henry Steele, as they walked out of the theater after seeing it. "It makes our pictures look silly!"

The picture was directed by Roberto Rossellini. Ingrid, like everyone else in the American film industry, had never heard of him before.

In October 1946, for the first time, Ingrid told her husband she wanted a divorce. He talked her out of it.

A month later she opened in *Joan of Lorraine* on Broadway to rave notices from the critics. But later, when Hollywood got its hands on the script for a screenplay, the spirit went out of the story. Ingrid's filmed *Joan of Arc* didn't measure up to her stage success. (It says something about the perceptions of Hollywood producers and directors that they have never been

Peter and 18-year-old Pia Lindstrom arrive at Idlewild (remember?) Airport. After a bitter estrangement, Pia and her mother had reconciled. *Wide World Photos*

Rossellini and Bergman on vacation. He had announced: "I'm going to put the horns on Mr. Bergman." *Wide World Photos*

able to do a successful picture about the Maid of Orleans.)

In the spring of 1948 she took a two-week vacation in New York. One afternoon she went to a movie. It was *Paisan,* and it consisted of six entirely separate incidents.

The director was Roberto Rossellini.

Afterwards she had dinner with Irene Selznick and told her how much she'd like to make a picture with a director capable of such work. Miss Selznick suggested that she write to Rossellini and tell him that. "He might get the wrong idea," Ingrid said. Miss Selznick reassured her. A few days later Lindstrom told his wife he saw nothing wrong with the idea.

So she sat down and wrote a letter:

"Dear Mr. Rossellini——

"I saw your films, *Open City* and *Paisan,* and enjoyed them very much. If you need a Swedish actress who speaks English very well, who has not forgotten her German, who is not very understandable in French, and who in Italian knows only 'ti amo,' I am ready to come and make a film with you.

"Best regards,
Ingrid Bergman"

The son of an architect, Roberto Rossellini was then forty-three years old. He had dissipated a legacy, worked as a racing driver and at odd jobs, then gone into films, first as a cutter and later as a director. He had also had one wife and innumerable mistresses.

But he had never had anything, anyone, of the stature of Ingrid Bergman, as actress, woman, or wife.

A cable arrived in America:

"Mrs. Ingrid Bergman:

"I have just received with great emotion your letter which happens to arrive on the anniversary of my birthday and the most precious gift. It is absolutely true that I dreamed to make a film with you and from this very moment I will do everything that such dream becomes reality as soon as possible. I will write you a long letter to submit to you my ideas. With my admiration please accept the expression of my gratitude together with my best regards.

Roberto Rossellini
Hotel Excelsior Rome"

The result of all this was that Ingrid Bergman, who was in London filming *Under Capricorn,* had a meeting in Paris with Rossellini, who went there during a lull in filming *The Miracle.* Lindstrom was there, too, and it was agreed that Ingrid would make a movie with Rossellini.

When he got back to Rome, Rossellini told his friends, "Swedish women are the easiest in the world to impress because they have such cold husbands. The love they get is an analgesic balm instead of a tonic."

The following January he flew to New York to accept the Film Critics' award for *Paisan* as the best foreign-language film to be shown during the year in the U.S. Before boarding the plane in Rome, he said to the people around him, "I'm going to put the horns on Mr. Bergman."

A portent of what was to come was Walter Winchell's exclusive tip on the radio: "Ingrid Bergman's one and only love is coming to Hollywood to see her!"

Rossellini was on a train bound for Los Angeles at that moment.

He stayed at the Lindstroms' home, by invitation of Ingrid and her husband, and she took him everywhere—to parties, to the beach, to unusual places— with her husband's explicit approval.

Then Rossellini flew back to Italy. Three weeks later, on March 20, Ingrid landed at Rome's airport. Rossellini's welcoming words were, *"Je t'aime"* (French for "I love you").

Their affair began almost immediately.

In a few days Ingrid wrote a letter to her husband, telling him about her passion for Rossellini and indicating her desire for a divorce. She gave the letter to Rossellini to read and mail. He not only read it, he even showed it to his friends, who numbered half of Rome. Soon everyone knew what it said:

"Petter *lilla* [little]——

"It will be very difficult for you to read this letter and it is difficult for me to write it. But I believe it is the only way. I would like to explain everything from the beginning, but you already know enough. And I would like to ask forgiveness, but that seems ridiculous.

"It was not altogether my fault, and how can you forgive that I went to stay with Roberto. I know he has also written you and told you all that there is to tell.

"It was not my intention to fall in love and go to Italy

forever. After all our plans and dreams, you know that is true. But how can I help it or change it? You saw in Hollywood how my enthusiasm for Roberto grew and grew, and you know how much alike we are, with the same desire for the same kind of work and the same understanding of life.

"I thought maybe I could conquer the feeling I had for him when I saw him in his own milieu, so different from mine. But it turned out just the opposite. The people, the life, the country is not strange. It is what I always wanted.

"I had not the courage to talk more about him at home than I did with you as it all seemed so incredible, like an adventure, and at the same time I didn't realize the depth of his feelings.

"*Min* [my] Petter, I know how this letter falls like a bomb on our house, our Pelle [a name they'd chosen for their next child], our future, our past so filled with sacrifice and help on your part.

"And now you stand alone in the ruins and I am unable to help you. *Stackars lilla pappa men also stackars lilla mama* [poor little papa, but also poor little mama].

"Mama"

And then the two, Ingrid and Roberto, cast caution to the winds and behaved for all the world to see like two lovers. On April 13 the first report of the affair appeared in the American press, cautiously phrased because of the fear of a libel suit. But the stories began to pour out of Italy in a torrent. As the lovers demonstrated their disregard for discretion, the news stories grew increasingly frank and detailed.

To an America which was used to thinking of Ingrid Bergman in her role as Joan of Arc, a holy creature, it was more than an offense against the moral code: it was virtually blasphemy.

Newspaper editorials and columnists condemned her. Clergymen preached sermons ripping into her as a symptom of the decaying morality of the postwar world. The usual bluenoses in the women's clubs, the civic groups, and self-appointed censorship groups called for a boycott of her films. It was a verbal lynching.

Lindstrom had a secret meeting with Ingrid at Messina. He

turned thumbs down on a divorce. He said she must finish the picture and return to Hollywood; then they'd discuss it.

The upshot of the meeting was a public statement by Ingrid in which she said that after finishing work on *Stromboli* she would "leave Italy and meet my husband either in Sweden or the United States."

The scandal—and the hue and cry—grew steadily worse. Finally Ingrid issued a public statement that she had asked her husband for a divorce.

Still the furor raged on. The Swedish newspapers now were saying that Ingrid was a disgrace to her homeland, abandoning her husband and child and making a public spectacle of herself with a notorious Italian roué. (That was the year Ingmar Bergman—no relation to Ingrid—made his first big film, *Thirst*, which would be followed by some of the most distinguished pictures ever made by a single director, movies which would reflect the increasing candor and honesty of society about sensuality.)

By November 1949 rumors were flying that Ingrid was pregnant. On December 12 Louella O. Parsons, the Hearst newspapers' saccharine-sounding but venomous Hollywood correspondent, broke the news:

INGRID BERGMAN BABY DUE
IN THREE MONTHS AT ROME

The fat was really in the fire.

On February 2, 1950, the baby, a boy they named Robertino, was born. On February 9 Ingrid got a Mexican divorce *in absentia*. But even then legal technicalities delayed the wedding of Ingrid and Rossellini. It was not until May 24 that they were able to get married and then it had to be a Mexican wedding by proxy, with the principals in Rome and the stand-ins in Juarez.

At last it appeared that Ingrid's life could settle into tranquility.

Lindstrom later got an American divorce, but the friction between him and Ingrid continued because of their disagreement over when or how she was to be permitted to see Pia, their daughter. Ingrid's lawyer went to court to try to improve her rights with respect to the girl, but the headlines after the hearing read: "I Don't Love My Mother, Pia Says." She said she didn't miss her mother and didn't have any desire to see

Ingrid with her children. When her marriage to Rossellini was annulled, Ingrid became Mrs. Lars Schmidt. That love-match was also destined for trouble.

Wide World Photos

her—statements that seemed forced and unlikely to many observers.

As was to be expected, Lindstrom won the court fight.

Five days earlier, on June 18, 1952, Ingrid had given birth to twin girls, Isabella and Isotta.

Stromboli had been an artistic and a box-office flop. Ingrid and her husband made five more pictures together; they were all very bad (including another attempt at putting Joan of Arc on film). It appeared that these two might make a great pair in love, but not in art.

In 1955 she did a film directed by Jean Renoir in Paris. The following year Darryl Zanuck, never one to pay much tribute to convention, had the courage to sign her to a contract to do a movie for him; it was *Anastasia*, which resulted in her second Oscar.

On December 1, 1956, she opened on the Paris stage in *Tea and Sympathy* and scored a tremendous hit. Indeed, Ingrid Bergman has probably been the only actress in the past quarter century who could, and did, appear on the stage and in films in several different countries, speaking the national tongue in each instance.

Away from Rossellini, Bergman was great; under his direction, her art was suppressed and destroyed, or so it seemed to many people. Indeed, it seemed, Rossellini, for he was quite transparently wild with jealousy and frustration at her success. A week after she opened in Paris, he left for India. As they parted, Ingrid knew it was the beginning of the end of their marriage.

In India, Rossellini made a movie and entered into a liaison with Sonali Das Gupta, a twenty-seven-year-old married woman who was a scriptwriter. *The New York Daily News* broke the story and disclosed that the woman was pregnant. It seemed like an old story.

In 1958 the marriage of Ingrid and Rossellini was annulled in Italy. On December 21 Ingrid was married to Swedish impresario Lars Schmidt in London, a union that was also destined for trouble.

In America, the tide of public opinion had finally turned. Ingrid Bergman, by now reconciled with daughter Pia, had been welcomed back to the U.S. with affection, respect, and even wild enthusiasm.

11 Lana Turner:
Death of a Playmate

Julia Jean Mildred Frances Turner was born in Wallace, a small mining town in Idaho, on February 8, 1920. Her father, John Virgil Turner, an itinerant miner, stevedore, and laborer, and her mother, Mildred, separated when the girl was seven, although she was not told of the breakup. She was sent to live with friends of her mother at Modesto, California. The family with whom she lived treated her "like a scullery maid," she later said. She had to get up early to make breakfast for the family, prepare the dinner before leaving for school, do the family laundry on Saturday and the ironing on Sunday. When the daughter of the house neglected a small household chore, the Turner girl was blamed; she was beaten with a stick until "my back was bruised and bleeding." It was the kind of mistreatment in childhood that often leads, psychologists say, to sadistic-masochistic attitudes toward sex and love when the child grows up.

On December 15, 1930, when the girl was ten, her father was murdered in San Francisco. He had just left a crap game the winner, and someone knew it. That someone cracked his skull

America's sweater girl in a nostalgic scene from her first movie, *They Won't Forget*. "She's not an actress, she's a commodity," Pauline Kael said later of the buxom blonde. *The Museum of Modern Art/Film Stills Archive*

from behind, robbed the fallen man, and left him to die in the night. The murder was never solved.

It was not until the murder that the girl learned that her parents had been separated. Her mother went to Modesto to break the news of the father's death. There she discovered how the child had been mistreated. (The child must also have felt rejected and abandoned, unloved and unworthy, one would think.) The mother decided to take the girl back to San Francisco with her.

It continued to be a bleak childhood. The mother, a hairdresser, made little money in those Depression days. Occasionally she was out of work, and she'd have to pawn some of the family's meager possessions for food money.

By January 1936 mother and daughter were living in Los Angeles. Her daughter was in high school or was supposed to be. But one Tuesday the girl played hooky, and what happened to her as a result has set back the cause of education a good many years.

She was "discovered."

The girl, by now a very curvesome young thing, was sipping a strawberry malt at the soda fountain in the Top Hat Malt Shop, at Sunset and Highland Avenues, when a man with a little black mustache, who had been looking at her for some time, approached her and asked, "How would you like to be in pictures?"

Now, even a sixteen-year-old girl knows how corny a line that is.

This was that rare time when the question was put in all seriousness, however. The man gave her his card and asked her to call him. The card identified him as William Wilkerson, editor and publisher of the *Hollywood Reporter*, a powerful motion picture trade journal.

The girl had been wearing a sweater in the malt shop. In her first picture, Mervyn Le Roy's *They Won't Forget*, an anti-lynching film which was one of Hollywood's infrequent forays into the hazards of realistic and courageous moviemaking, the second scene showed her in a sweater hurrying along a crowded street. The girl was embarrassed by her appearance when the scene was shown ("I looked so *cheap!*" she cried), but it produced a name that shot her to fame almost instantly.

She became "The Sweater Girl."

The very day that scene was filmed, the girl went with

Wilkerson to the Zeppo Marx talent agency. (Zeppo was the straight man and romantic lead in the first five Marx Brothers film comedies. He left his brothers' act after *Duck Soup,* in 1933, to become a talent agent.) At the agency Mervyn Le Roy was waiting for her. For half an hour they sat around trying to think of a first name for the fledgling actress. None of her real names would do, of course; in those days it was the ultimate in heresy to suggest that a film actress' real name would go very well on a theater marquee. Finally, out of the blue, the girl herself suggested Lana. Everyone accepted it at once.

A star had been born: Lana Turner.

In the years that followed, she made innumerable movies, none of them very good. (Twenty years later she finally won an Academy Award nomination, but not the Oscar, for her acting in *Peyton Place.*)

She managed to keep in the headlines with her marriages and her romances, which were more numerous than those of most Hollywood stars. Her first husband was bandleader Artie Shaw, whom she married on their first date. She was engaged to attorney Greg Bautzer at the time, but she became annoyed at him for calling off a date, so she eloped with Shaw. That marriage lasted four months.

Then came Stephen Crane, an actor, whom she married in 1943, after a month of dating him. But it turned out that Crane's divorce from his first wife was not yet final when he married Lana. She was forced to get an annulment of the invalid marriage. Then she found she was pregnant. She remarried Crane. A year after the child was born, Lana divorced him.

Husband No. 3 was playboy socialite Henry J. (Bob) Topping, who had just gotten a divorce from Arlene Judge. (*That* had been quite a marriage, even for Hollywood. When Arlene and Bob married, she became—now follow this carefully—her ex-husband's sister-in-law and he became step-father to his nephew. Probably the genealogists didn't care.) That marriage lasted four and half years. It ended in Nevada in 1952.

The fourth man to risk the perils of matrimony with Lana was Lex Barker, who was one of the men who portrayed Tarzan on the screen. In 1953 he became Lana's husband and in 1957 he joined the growing club of her ex-husbands.

In between the husbands there were many less formal

Cheryl, who adored Johnny, met the re-united couple at the airport when they returned from their holiday in Mexico. Two weeks later Johnny was dead and Cheryl was charged with murder.

United Press International Photo

Lana, Cheryl, and father Stephen Crane as they left police station. "Daddy, daddy, come quick!" she had said on the phone. After the trial, Lana lost custody of the girl.

Los Angeles Times Photo

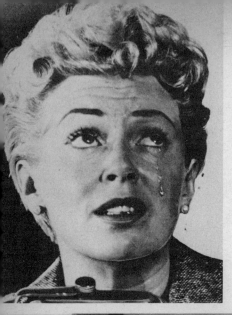

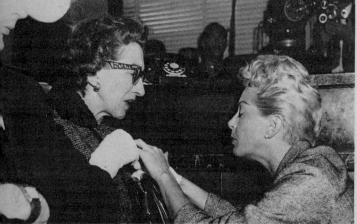

During a recess at the inquest, Lana knelt at her mother's knee for encouragement. None of her soap opera roles equalled this real-life drama, and her movies did better than ever at the box office.

mother's knee: Wide World Photos
with tear: Los Angeles Times Photo

attachments. "Let's be honest," Lana once said, "the physical attracts me first. Then, if you get to know the man's mind and soul and heart, that's icing on the cake."

The list of men in her life was like a telephone book. They included Turhan Bey, Robert Hutton, Rory Calhoun, John Dall, Frank Sinatra, Howard Hughes, Tyrone Power.

After she shed Lex Barker, however, Lana was temporarily manless. One day she got a telephone call.

And the greatest drama of her life began.

The voice on the other end of the wire said his name was Johnny Stompanato. They had some mutual friends. He'd like a date.

It seems incredible, but he got it.

Stompanato had been born at Woodstock, Illinois, in 1925, although he didn't tell Lana that; he led her to believe he was ten years older than his actual age, so she wouldn't realize that he was younger than she. In 1943 he had graduated from Kemper Military School at Bonneville, Missouri. After that he went briefly to Notre Dame University before entering the Marine Corps in 1944. In 1947 he was discharged from the service. During that time he had somehow managed to get married and divorced twice.

Hollywood is a great place for a guy on the make, and Johnny was on the make when he got out of the service. He went to Los Angeles. There, in 1948, he got together with gangster Mickey Cohen, who had just taken over California for the national crime syndicate following the murder of the previous crime boss, Bugsy Siegel. By all accounts, it was an order from Lucky Luciano that led to Siegel's being murdered in the living room of his inamorata, Virginia Hill, at 810 Linden Drive in Beverly Hills.

Organized crime had been mixing with the film colony for a long time, at least as far back as the early 1920s, when Wallace Reid became a junkie. Although the close relationships of George Raft and Frank Sinatra to gangsters has been well known, many others in the motion picture industry also were willing to accept mobsters on a social basis. Jean Harlow, for example, was godmother to two of Bugsy Siegel's children. When the district attorney's men once wanted to take Siegel in for questioning, they found him at a party in Beverly Hills, at the home of studio head Jack Warner. In 1945, when Siegel began building the first big Las Vegas gambling hotel, the Flamingo, the mob money, one-fourth of the shares, more or less, was held by Wilkerson, the *Hollywood Reporter* publisher. The pattern of curious associations of names of film stars and mobsters continues to this day. As recently as 1967 a federal grand jury reported that big-time bookmaker Frank Erickson of New York had given Mafia leaders Jerry Catena, Tommy Eboli, and Pasquale Eboli gift memberships in—of all things!—the Mount Kenya Safari Club of Africa; one of the club's three co-owners is movie star William Holden.

Apparently Johnny Stompanato's first job for Mickey Cohen was bodyguard. Later he began to operate on his own, that is, with more autonomy, as an agent of Cohen. The Kefauver Committee took a considerable interest in the affairs of the two men when that Senate group was investigating organized crime, but the panel was not able to establish very much beyond the fact that Cohen and Stompanato frequently exchanged sums of money that Cohen insisted were loans, involving as much as $4,000.

Committee counsel Rudolph Halley suggested that Stompanato might be getting his money through blackmail, one of the favorite rackets of the Los Angeles mobsters for many years.

"Not him," said Cohen. "Those stories are made up. He was the kind of guy that never even beat up a dame. If he got into trouble, I'd have to protect him."

After Stompanato's death, his brother visited Beverly Hills Police Chief Clinton H. Anderson. He was anxious to get "some unidentified missing property" of Stompanato. Anderson gave him the address he had for the dead man—the De Capri Hotel in West Los Angeles.

But Stompanato's apartment had been broken into a few hours after his death was announced in the press. Someone—it was never discovered who that person was—had ransacked the place. What they were looking for, and whether they found it, is anybody's guess.

A few days later a friend of Stompanato went to Anderson's office and gave him a little wooden box. Stompanato, not trusting his underworld associates, had given it to a "clean" friend to keep for him. In the box the police found a .32 caliber snub-nosed revolver, bank books, personal papers, and rolls of film negatives. "Printed and enlarged," Anderson disclosed in *Beverly Hills Is My Beat,* his memoirs, "the negatives revealed pictures of nude women in compromising situations.

Some of the pictures had apparently been taken while the victims were unaware they were being photographed, and they were recognizable. The pictures would have been a gold mine for a blackmailer." Anderson, for obvious reasons, did not identify any of the women in the photos.

Anderson says that the police had been watching Stompanato's activities with interest for years. The police "knew he had obtained large sums of money from individuals who were afraid to complain to the police, and we were aware that he had accepted money from a number of his women friends."

Tall, handsome, dark in hair and skin, Johnny was fairly obvious, almost a caricature of a gigolo. He liked to wear his shiny silk shirts open to the belt, displaying his manly torso. In short, he was the beach athlete type, scarcely the person one would expect a movie queen to fall for. But many women who were rich and famous succumbed to his somewhat dubious charms.

One might expect a woman in Lana Turner's position to investigate any man who attempted to become a close friend, and the most cursory check would have turned up the fact that Stompanato was, to put it mildly, unsavory. But Lana probably knew that anyhow. It has been reported that she first heard of him through Mickey Cohen himself. Movie stars have long been suckers for gangsters, and Lana appears to have been attracted by them, like so many others.

Cheryl Crane, Lana's daughter, liked Stompanato. Cheryl, the offspring of Lana's second marriage, had had to adapt herself to many situations in her young life (she was fourteen when Stompanato died). She had grown up in a succession of private schools, private camps, ranches. She had never had a chance to be close to her mother, who was too eager seeking affection to bestow it.

The fourteen months during which her mother saw Johnny Stompanato were a happy time, by and large, for Cheryl. She had never had so much attention paid to her. She went horseback riding with Johnny, swimming with him, and so on. When he and Lana were off somewhere, it was to Johnny that Cheryl wrote most often, tossing in a line asking how her mother was. And when Cheryl was off somewhere with Lana, a very unusual circumstance, the girl always wrote to Stompanato.

"Johnny and the kid was like that," said Mickey Cohen later, crossing his fingers. "She was crazy about him."

This was one of Cheryl's letters to Stompanato in 1957:

"Dear Johnny——

"First of all, please excuse this paper but it's really all I have right now.

"I just got your letter this morning because I was home for the weekend.

"How have you been? And how is mother?

"Rowena [a mare owned by Cheryl] is just fine. I'm not afraid of her any more and she acts just like she used to last summer. Yes, I still want to take her to Estes Park this summer. I thought for a while I wouldn't be able to handle her but now I know I can.

"School is just fine, but not getting any easier. I went to see Johnny Mathis at the Crescendo Sunday nite and he was terrific. Have you been doing any water skiing lately? Please do, and think of me. I love it. When are you all coming back? Soon, I hope.

                                        "Love ya,
                                              Cheri"

Her mother's letters to Stompanato from London, where she was making a movie, a few weeks later were not terribly restrained. These are typical excerpts:

"Sweetheart, please keep well, because I need you so—and so you will always be strong and able to caress me, hold me, tenderly at first, and crush me into your very own being. . . ."

"My Beloved Love, just this morning your precious exciting letter arrived. . . . Every line warms me and makes me ache and miss you each tiny moment—and it's true—it's beautiful, yet terrible. But, just so is deep love. . . . Hold me, dear lover. . . ."

"I'm your woman and I need you, my man! To love and be loved by—don't ever doubt or forget that. . . ."

" 'My romance,' hah! It's a hell of a lot more than that! That's for sure. . . . There's so much to say—but it's easier when you're holding me all through the night.' And we can either whisper, or shout, or scream our love for each other to each other. . . . And oh, so many, many kisses—so fierce that they hurt me. . . ."

Lana's letters became more and more importunate. She couldn't wait to get home to Johnny. She had to have him with her at once, in London.

So Stompanato borrowed a couple of thousand dollars from Mickey Cohen and flew to London.

At first the reunion was everything that Lana had promised herself it would be. In Johnny's arms her hungers were satisfied. But not all of his, it seemed.

They began to argue about money. She had almost always picked up the tab, and she had given him $10,000 on one occasion. But now he wanted her to buy a story on which to base a screenplay. The "earnest money" was $1,000, but Lana wouldn't put it up because her financial advisers frowned on it.

This was especially painful to Johnny because he'd begun to develop acting ambitions. It had been his idea to star in the movie.

Finally they had an argument so violent that Lana became frightened. He threatened to disfigure her or cripple her.

"After he had choked me and thrown me down," she later recalled, "he went into the bathroom and he got a razor and he came and grabbed my head, all the time screaming at me violent things. Then he said that it may only start with a little one now, just give me a taste of it, and even so, he would do worse. I pleaded. I said I would do anything, anything, just please don't hurt me. [I said,] 'If you claim to love me, how can you hurt me? Please don't.'

"As he let go of me, he said, 'That's just to let you know I am not kidding. Don't think you can ever get away.'"

The frightened actress told her director, who asked Scotland Yard to handle the matter in such a way as to avoid publicity. The Scotland Yard men escorted Stompanato to a plane and made sure he went back to the U.S.

But after Lana returned to the States, there was a reconciliation, and she and Stompanato went off to Acapulco for a seven-week vacation. Later she was to say that she was terribly afraid of him then, but the people who saw them in Mexico at the time didn't believe it. They said it was Lana who kept pursuing Johnny, not the other way around.

Her water skiing instructor said Lana didn't like Johnny to talk to anyone else. The skipper of the yacht *Rose Maria*, on which Lana and Johnny spent nearly half their time at Acapulco, said, "I couldn't understand why a movie queen

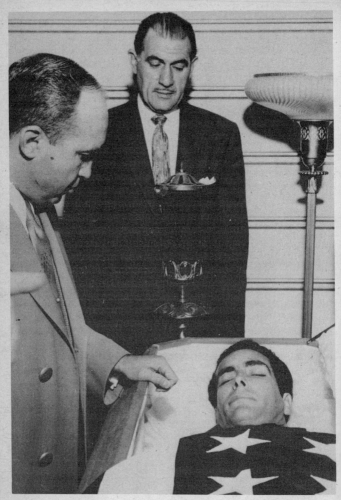

Gangster Mickey Cohen viewing the body of his former bodyguard. Annoyed at being stuck with Johnny's funeral expenses, Cohen released Lana's torrid love letters to the press. *Wide World Photos*

would have to keep on chasing after him. But no matter what he was doing on board, she was at his side. He would be sitting in a deck chair and she would come along and all of a sudden sit right down in his lap without being asked."

Finally the Mexican idyll was at an end, and the two headed back to Hollywood—and death.

On April 4,1958, Stephen Crane, who had long since abandoned acting in order to become the owner of a restaurant called the Luau, was at his establishment when he got a message that there was a telephone call for him. When he reached the phone, he heard Cheryl's voice:

"Daddy, Daddy, come quick! Something terrible has happened!"

"What's the matter?" he asked.

"Don't ask any questions, Daddy—just hurry, *please!*"

Crane didn't have his car at the restaurant. He asked a friend, who was at the bar, to drive him. They sped to 730 North Bedford Drive in Beverly Hills. As Crane leaped from the car, Cheryl called out from the doorway:

"Daddy!"

"Yes, I'm coming," he called, sprinting up the driveway.

Cheryl turned and ran.

"Wait a minute, baby," her father called out.

He caught up with her and they ran up the stairs together to the second floor. Lana was there.

"Something terrible has happened," she said.

He looked past her into the bedroom on the right. A man was lying there on the floor on his back.

"What happened, Cherie?" Crane asked his daughter.

"I did it, Daddy," she said, "but I didn't mean to. He was going to hurt Mommy."

She was sobbing, her adolescent body wracked with her anguish. "I didn't mean to, I didn't mean to," she kept sobbing.

"I know you didn't," Lana said, putting her arms around the girl.

"I just wanted to protect you," Cheryl stammered between sobs, as her mother and father tried to comfort her.

Two doctors were summoned. As they began working over Stompanato, they ordered an ambulance. The cop on the beat arrived then and called his headquarters to give the alarm. Before Chief Anderson could arrive, attorney Jerry Giesler was on the scene. Somebody in the family had summoned him.

The investigation disclosed that there had been a wild quarrel between Lana and Johnny. It had begun because he was jealous, or so she said, of her plans to have dinner with some friends a few days later without him. But another cause was her discovery that he had lied about his age, that he was actually five years younger than she.

About 8:30 p.m. Stompanato, who had spent the afternoon with Lana, returned to the house and resumed the fight. Lana walked into Cheryl's room and he followed her, "saying some very bad things . . . the language was bad, swearing." She told him she'd warned him not to talk like that "in front of the baby." She walked out of the room and downstairs, with the hoodlum following her, shouting.

"I——I——I was just finding out too many lies," she later said, at the inquest, "and that this one more that I had found out was just not the worst lie."

She told Johnny, "I can't go on like this. I have begged, I have pleaded for you to leave me alone."

They went back upstairs, Lana saying, "There's no use discussing it any further; I can't go on like this and I want you to leave me alone."

(All of this disagrees with the statements from Acapulco, but the only one who could dispute the matter, Stompanato himself, was beyond caring.)

This is Lana's story of what happened after that, as told at the inquest:

"He grabbed me by the arms . . . and started shaking me and cursing me very badly, and saying that, as he had told me before, no matter what I did, how I tried to get away, he would never leave me, that if he said jump, I would jump; if he said hop, I would hop; and I would have to do anything and everything he told me or he'd cut my face or cripple me.

"And if—when—if it went beyond that, he would kill me, and my daughter, and my mother. And he said it did not matter what, he would get me where it would hurt the most, and that would be my daughter and my mother.

"I broke away from his holding my—holding me, and I turned around to face the door, and my daughter was stand-

ing there. And I said, 'Please, Cheryl, please don't listen to any
of this. I beg you to go back to your room.'

"She looked at me, and I think that—as if to say, 'Are you
sure, Mother?' Because I know I repeated it, and I begged her.
I said, 'Please, Cheryl, don't listen to this. I beg you to go back
to your room.'

"I turned to Mr. Stompanato after I had closed the door, and
I said, 'That's just great, my child had to hear all that, the
horrible——And I can't go through anymore.'

"And he kept swearing and threatening me, and he had had
a jacket and a shirt hanging in the closet. I forget exactly when
it was there or if he had brought another change from his
apartment. Anyway, it was hanging there and he walked away
from me and went to the closet, and it was on a hanger. And
he walked back to me and was holding the jacket on the
hanger in a way that he was going to strike me with it.

"And I said, 'Don't—don't ever touch me again. I am—I am
absolutely finished. This is the end. And I want you to get out.'

"And after I said that, I was walking toward the bedroom
door, and he was right behind me, and I opened it, and my
daughter came in.

"I swear it was so fast, I—I truthfully thought she had hit him
in the stomach. The best I can remember, they came together
and they parted. I still never saw a blade.

"Mr. Stompanato grabbed himself here [indicating]. . . . And
he started to move forward, and he made almost a half turn,
and then dropped on his back, and when he dropped, his
arms went out, so that I still did not see that there was blood or
a wound until I ran over to him, and I saw his sweater was cut,
and I lifted the sweater up and I saw his wound.

"I remember only barely hearing my daughter sobbing and I
ran into my bathroom, which is very close, and I grabbed a
towel. I didn't know what to do.

"And then I put the towel there, and Mr. Stompanato was
making very dreadful sounds in his throat of gasping—terrible
sounds—and I went to the telephone and I called my mother
because I had been out of the country for so long, and I could
not remember my doctor's number."

But Johnny Stompanato, gangster, lady-killer, blackmailer,
was beyond the help of any doctor. The knife that Cheryl had
run down to the kitchen to get had dealt him a mortal blow.

Whether she had plunged the knife into his abdomen or whether he had run upon the knife in pursuing Lana is a question that even Lana and Cheryl, who were there, apparently couldn't answer.

But certainly the wound was one that an army of doctors could not repair in time. The knife had slashed through the abdominal wall, the liver, and up through the aorta, the main artery.

Stompanato's brother charged that the whole story didn't come out at the inquest, and many of the dead man's hoodlum friends felt the same way. Some indicated doubt that the fourteen-year-old girl had held the knife, but they overlooked the fact that this girl already was more than five feet eight inches tall. Others suggested that the real cause of the quarrel had not been disclosed; they hinted that Stompanato had been paying too much attention to Cheryl herself.

But none of those challenges to the official story was justified by the facts made public at the inquest.

Some additional facts might have come out if a damage suit, filed on behalf of Stompanato's son against Lana, Crane, and Cheryl, had been permitted to go to trial. The suit asserted that doubt existed over whether Cheryl or Lana wielded the eight-inch knife and whether Stompanato might not have been killed "willfully and intentionally." But the suit was settled out of court for $20,000.

For the many Hollywood victims of the mob's blackmailers, there must have been considerably sardonic pleasure in observing the hoodlums' indignation and outrage. The blackmail racket does not operate on the assumption that a predator will end up being a victim.

The scandal didn't hurt Lana's career. Indeed, it helped her. Her pictures, which were released at the rate of almost one a year over the next decade, did better at the box office than ever before. Even the usually hyper-sensitive television network executives acknowledged that the American public approved of her when they starred her in a 1969 TV series, *The Survivors*.

She lost custody of Cheryl, who was put in the care of Lana's mother. Cheryl was hard to keep in hand, and the courts soon decided that she should be sent to El Retiro School for Girls, a shelter for problem girls located in the San Fernando Valley. But Cheryl ran away from El Retiro twice, so it was decided she might do better in a private school. By 1961 the courts were willing to let her go home to live with her mother.

In the 1970s Cheryl was working as a hostess in a restaurant owned by her father. She was living alone, and had not married.

A fictional version of the case, thinly disguised, was filmed in 1964 under the title, *Where Love Has Gone*.

James Dougherty, a 21-year-old aircraft worker, married the sexy teen-ager and took her to Catalina. She was Norma Jean to him.

The Museum of Modern Art / Film Stills Archive

12 Marilyn Monroe:
Death and the Kennedy Connection

Marilyn Monroe was the epitome of the movie star. In each generation there is just one star who outshines all the others with a brilliance beyond comparison. It's a difficult phenomenon to explain. Perhaps Marilyn herself put it best when she observed, ''You're always running into people's unconscious.''

The big star isn't usually the best actor or actress, nor the smartest, nor even the most attractive. There is some indefinable quality that arouses a special kind of interest and enthusiasm in the audience. Mary Pickford was the first star of this magnitude. After her came Clara Bow. Then Jean Harlow. Then there was a hiatus of about a decade—probably because of the war—before the next queen came along: Marilyn Monroe.

It is nothing short of miraculous that Marilyn Monroe ever emerged on the screen. Everything was against her from birth and even before. Both of her grandparents on her mother's side had to be committed to insane asylums. An uncle killed himself. Her mother became psychotic and had to be hospitalized five years after the girl's birth; she was still in custodial care when Marilyn Monroe was buried.

As for her father, he was as nebulous as the fathers of most illegitimate offspring. When Marilyn was born in Los Angeles General Hospital on June 1, 1926, her name was listed as Norma Jean Mortenson, but her mother was listed as Mrs. Gladys Baker, age twenty-four. Marilyn didn't know she was a bastard until she was sixteen, when she applied for a marriage license. After she became a star, she began a search for her father, with the aid of private detectives and newspaper stories. Whether she ever found him is a question that probably never will be answered. In 1929 an Edward Mortenson was killed in a motorcycle accident in Youngstown, Ohio; Marilyn was told he had been her father. But in 1950 she was told that he was a well-to-do dairy farmer who lived about 150 miles south of Los Angeles; she talked to him on the telephone once, but he refused to see her. As her drama coach, Natasha Lytess, who was present, recalled, "She pleaded with him to let her see him. He refused. She gave him her telephone number. He never called." (There are reports, not too reliable, that he did call finally, when he was on his death bed in 1962, but Marilyn refused to talk to him.)

There were still other candidates for the honor. On one occasion Marilyn was told that a Los Angeles civic leader was her father. At still another time, Grace McKee, her mother's closest friend, told her that it was still another man, that he was still alive, and that he had wanted to adopt his unsanctified offspring but Marilyn's mother wouldn't let him because she hated him so. It is even possible that Marilyn's mother really didn't know who her father was; she appears to have been fairly generous with her favors, at least in the year or two just before Norma Jean's birth.

Whoever Norma Jean's father was, Marilyn Monroe never stopped searching for him, in both a real and a psychological sense. She never stopped feeling the pain of his loss, the terrible need for him. She tried to find him in men, and failed.

Yet there is a kind of awful appropriateness in her lack of a father. Her mother worked in the film industry as a film cutter at Columbia and RKO-Radio. Perhaps—certainly in a symbolic sense—the motion picture industry itself fathered this beautiful girl, by a kind of cultural parthenogenesis. Marilyn herself seems to have felt this; the day before she died *Life* magazine carried an interview in which she said, "The industry should behave like a mother whose child has just run out in front of a car. But instead of clasping the child to them, they start punishing the child."

The movies were the only bright spot in the pathetic life of Norma Jean Baker, the name under which she was carried on the Los Angeles welfare rolls. She was a ward of the county, which paid twenty dollars a month to foster parents to take care of her. In the memory of the adult Marilyn Monroe, there was an almost constantly changing succession of foster homes, although investigators later could find records of only three (there could have been more). There were enough to rob the girl of any sense of security. "I guess I wanted love more than anything else in the world at that time," Marilyn later said.

She didn't find it.

When she was seven, she made the mistake of calling a foster mother "Mama," but the woman sharply rebuked her. The woman snapped, "I'm not your Mama. I'm not related to you at all. You just board out here."

Marilyn herself once wrote a vivid account of the confusion and wretchedness of it all. "What one family would tell me was wrong, another family would tell me was right," she said. "One place where I lived they made me recite and sign a pledge: 'I promise, God helping me, not to buy, drink, sell, or give alcoholic liquor while I live; from all tobaccoes I'll abstain and never take God's name in vain.' Another family let me have empty liquor bottles to play with. Still another family made me pray every night that I wouldn't wake up in hell. I always felt insecure and in the way. But most of all, I just felt scared."

All the nameless fears and anxieties were multiplied, mixed up, augmented, and spread in shrieking colors on the quivering fabric of her mind like a nightmare montage by an event that occurred—or may have occurred—sometime in her childhood. It happened in one of her foster homes, which happened to be a rooming house. One night, when little Norma Jean was putting away some linens, one of the boarders, an elderly relatively prosperous man who wore dark suits, a gold watch and chain, and an Elk's tooth, motioned to her that he wanted her to come to him. Wonderingly, she went to the door of his room. He took her hand, smilingly, led her into the room, and closed the door, bolting it. He took off his coat and vest, hung them up carefully, sat down in a chair, and told the little girl to come and sit on his lap. He told her they'd play a little game.

He raped her.

Afterwards, the shaking child tried to tell her foster mother about it, although she'd been given a nickel to keep her mouth shut. But her foster mother called her a liar and slapped her across the mouth. Ever afterwards Norma Jean Mortenson stammered.

This is the story that Marilyn Monroe told many people. She told one that it happened when she was six. On another occasion she gave her age at the time as eight. Sometimes she said nine or eleven. Maybe it didn't happen at all; people sometimes have fantasies about childhood rape that are as real as life. Whether it did or didn't actually occur is really immaterial; reality or fantasy, it exerted a powerful influence on the rest of her life.

In the gothic terror-world of her childhood, the movies beckoned brightly, like a fairy godmother to Cinderella. "When I was five," she once told *Life*, "I think that's when I started wanting to be an actress—I loved to play. . . . When I was older I used to go to Grauman's Chinese Theater and try to fit my foot in the prints in the cement there. And I'd say, 'Oh, oh, my foot's too big. I guess that's out. . . .' It was the creative part that kept me going—trying to be an actress. I enjoy acting when you really hit it right. And I guess I've always had too much fantasy to be only a housewife."

She lived on movie fan magazines. She read them avidly and "believed every word of them," as she later said. Her favorite star, inevitably, was Jean Harlow, whom she would one day succeed as No. 1 sex symbol. (Indeed, Norma Jean's name was taken by her mother from the first names of Jean Harlow and Norma Talmadge.)

Until she was twelve the future sex queen of the cinema was so skinny and sexless that she was called "Norma Jean, the Human Bean," and she even played a boy's part in a drama production at Van Nuys High School. Then, one day, she borrowed a white sweater to wear to school. It happened to be a size or two smaller than she usually wore her sweaters. It made such a marked impression on the other kids at school that the following day Norma Jean experimented with makeup. "My arrival in school with painted lips, and darkened brows, and still encased in the magic sweater, started everybody buzzing," she recalled.

She told *Life* how everything was transformed for her at that time:

"Suddenly everything opened up. Even the girls paid a little attention to me, just because they thought, 'Hmmm, she's to be dealt with!' And I had this long walk to school, two and a half miles to school and two and a half miles back—it was just sheer pleasure. Every fellow honked his horn—you know, workers driving to work, waving, you know, and I'd wave back. The world became friendly."

Too friendly for the peace of mind of her legal guardian, and of the woman with whom Norma Jean was living at the time. They decided she had altogether too much sex appeal, and too much willingness to go more than halfway to get together with boys and men who showed an interest in her. The safest thing seemed to them to get her out of circulation.

So a marriage was arranged for her. The groom was James Dougherty, twenty-one, an aircraft worker who was dark and handsome. "We were introduced by her foster aunt," he once said. "We went out together about six months before we got married. Being an actress wasn't even on her mind then."

Eighteen days after her sixteenth birthday, the marriage took place. The date was June 19, 1942. They had an argument on their wedding night because Jim didn't like the way she had joined a conga line in a nightclub while celebrating the wedding, nor the way the men had admired her. Two years later Dougherty joined the Merchant Marine and was assigned to Catalina Island, where Norma Jean lived with him. She was still wearing tight sweaters and slacks, the men were still watching her, and Dougherty was still getting upset about it. Then Dougherty was shipped overseas and Norma Jean became a photographer's model.

Like so many of the major events in Norma Jean's life, it began accidentally. With her husband overseas, the young Mrs. Dougherty had gone to work in the plant of the Radio Plane Parts Company in Burbank, which was engaged in war production. One day in 1945 the Army sent photographer David Conover to the plant to take pictures to lift the morale of the soldiers overseas. She had a sweater—a tight one, of course—in her locker. She looked so good in the pictures that Conover told her she ought to be a professional model. She promptly signed up with the Blue Books Model Agency.

One day Andre de Dienes, who later came to be a well-known photographer, put in a call to the agency for a model.

Later that day the bell rang at his apartment in the famous Garden of Allah apartment house. "There came this lovely little girl in a pink sweater and checkered slacks,' he said after her death. "Right away I fell in love with this girl."

She told him that she was married, but her husband was away in the Merchant Marine. She didn't love her husband, she said.

Andre and Norma Jean went on a month-long trip up the coast. She posed for his camera against every conceivable kind of background—rocks, waters, snow, mountains, highways. He found that she was a good worker, but not strong. "She was frail, mentally and physically," he said. She had no defenses against the brutalities of the world. It was a quality that the other men in her life—and there were so many, so very many, of them—would not comment upon; many of them would use it to take advantage of her. "She was a sensitive, sweet little girl," Andre summed up.

Andre had to go to New York on business. By that time, he and Marilyn were lovers. While he was away, she went to Las Vegas. There, on October 2, 1946, she obtained a divorce from Dougherty. Two men were in for a jolt. Dougherty first got word of the divorce in a letter from his young wife's attorney. "It reached me in Yangtze," he said. "I was kind of shook up at that. . . . I sent a cablegram cancelling my allotment to her, and I went to Shanghai and had a ball." Andre de Dienes headed back to the West Coast after an absence of five months. "I phoned from New Mexico," he told a friend, "and she said, 'Andre, please don't come. I can't marry you. Forgive me.' "

When de Dienes arrived in Hollywood, he made a discreet inquiry or two. He found she was involved with someone else. "I knew it was all over," he said.

De Dienes's photos had been appearing in all the meh's magazines. Howard Hughes, the indefatigable "discoverer" of appetizing women, happened to see one of them. It was rumored that he directed the attention of the studios to Norma Jean, but Ben Lyon at 20th Century-Fox was the person who arranged for her first screen test.

The cameraman was Leon Shamroy. He never forgot tha test. "I got a cold chill," he said. "This girl had something hadn't seen since silent pictures. She had a kind of fantastic beauty like Gloria Swanson, when a movie star had to look

Marilyn and Joe Di Maggio waiting to get married. He neglected her for poker, baseball and t.v., but in his way he never stopped loving her.   *Wide World Photos*

beautiful, and she got sex on a piece of film like Jean Harlow. This is the first girl who looked like one of those lush stars of the silent era.''

It was Lyon who gave Norma Jean her new name, after 20th Century-Fox signed her. ''I told him that my mother's maiden name was Monroe and said that I had always liked that name,'' Marilyn later explained. ''Besides, I am a direct descendant of President Monroe. [Like most of Marilyn's statements, that was more likely wish than reality.] 'All right, Monroe's it,' he said. 'Now a first name. You're a remarkable combination of two different people I knew very well, Jean Harlow and Marilyn Miller. Marilyn sounds better with Monroe than Jean. That's it: Marilyn Monroe.' ''

She had the name, but not the fame. Her contract with 20th Century-Fox, she later said, ''was like my first vaccination—it didn't take.'' She only got a one-word walk-on in one movie, and that ended up on a cutting room floor. After six months her option was picked up and she got a salary boost to $150 a week, but six months later she was dropped from the studio's rolls.

Then she enrolled in the Actors' Lab, a workshop for aspiring young men and women. Her instructor there conceded later that she'd never have expected Marilyn to make the big time. She never spoke, not once, except in answer to questions or to read lines.

After ten months in limbo, Marilyn got another contract in March 1948. Max Arnow of Columbia Pictures had seen her first screen test, done for 20th Century-Fox, and had been impressed. Arnow arranged for Natasha Lytess to be her dramatic coach. Marilyn played a burlesque stripper and sang a few songs in a grade-B movie called *Ladies of the Chorus*. But when her contract ran out, Columbia dropped Marilyn, too.

During this time, inevitably, Marilyn had been meeting men. As she later told it, one studio boss suggested a party for two on his yacht; Marilyn turned down the proposition and failed to get a contract with his studio. Two days later, broke and desperate, she posed for a nude photograph for Tom Kelley. She got fifty dollars for photographs that would one day make a calendar a collectors' item.

To those who knew her in those days, the story of the calendar nude rang true, but the rejection of the yachting tryst seemed one of Marilyn's typical concoctions. It wasn't exactly that she lied, at least not in a hypocritical way. It was just that she liked to tell people what she thought they wanted to hear. And the public, she was sure, wanted to hear how demure and decorous she had been.

In fact, she had been anything but decorous and demure. The studio bosses, producers, directors—all the movie industry men she met at the time, or a great many of them—wanted to hear her say Yes, so she said it. There is ample evidence that she quickly lost the inhibitions about sex that Andre de Dienes had found her to have when they first became lovers on that month-long trip. Men who slept with her later—and there were a great many of them—found her capable of enjoying sex, willing, but not very imaginative. That was true even after she became the biggest of stars: she went on bedding men with very little hesitation, but she still wasn't very expert in bed. At the peak of her career she went to bed with a very famous male star, and told a friend the next day, "You know, I'm still not sure I'm doing it right." But she was almost always ready to do "it." She was like the girl who says, "Why shouldn't I go to bed with the guy? He really wants it so much, and it's no big deal to me." (An attitude that clearly reflected her lack of self-esteem, her feeling that she—and therefore her body—was basically worthless. This was an attitude that a childhood like hers might have instilled in any woman. The ruthless use of her body by so many men high in the film industry could only make her feel that they, too, regarded her as simply "a piece of meat.")

She enjoyed sex. She was uninhibited about it. She permitted her body to be used by men who made no attempt to conceal the fact that they felt not the slightest affection for her, or even interest in her; if anything, their attitude conveyed contempt. And somewhere, deep in her soul, Marilyn—although she went along with their demands in a passive way—harbored a resentment that would grow into a hatred and eventually compel her to fight back the only way a girl who couldn't say No could fight: by costing them money—by being so late that production schedules on her movies would always be meaningless, that costs would overrun budgets to an absurd degree, that producers and studio bosses would get ulcers from worrying about whether and when she would show up on a set.

Joseph M. Schenck, chairman of the board at 20th Century-Fox, met her and began inviting her to his home. She later said, "I know the word around Hollywood was I was Joe Schenck's girl friend, but that's a lie. I went to his house because I liked Mr. Schenck and I liked his food and it was better than Studio Club food." (She was living at the Studio Club then.) Schenck told Ezra Goodman, "She used to come here quite often for dinner. I think she liked to eat. We have good food here. No, I never had any romantic thoughts about Marilyn and she never had any such thoughts about me."

Perhaps they weren't romantic thoughts, but nobody who knew Marilyn at the time believed that she was going to Schenck's house for innocent reasons.

Johnny Hyde, executive vice-president of the influential William Morris Agency, was fifty-three (to her twenty-two) and married, but he became her acknowledged lover. He wanted to marry her. In those days he became the one person with any expertise and authority who encouraged her and praised her talents. "Isn't it sad," Marilyn said to Maurice Zolotow, "here's Johnny in love with me and I didn't return his love? But Johnny was kind to me and I was faithful to him." She was living with Hyde when he died—she wouldn't marry him,

Marilyn clung to the arm of attorney Jerry Geisler after her divorce from Joe. "A sex symbol becomes a thing," she said before her death. "I just hate being a thing."

Los Angeles Times Photo

although he was a millionaire—and his family ordered her out of Hyde's house within hours of his death. (He separated from his wife after meeting Marilyn.)

Friends like Schenck and Hyde were very powerful boosts to a girl with ambition in Hollywood.

Arthur Hornblow, Jr., and John Huston were looking for a blonde to play Louis Calhern's girl friend in *The Asphalt Jungle.* Lucille Ryman, casting agent for Metro-Goldwyn-Mayer, was helping in the hunt. She saw that first screen test of Marilyn's (Marilyn certainly got a lot of mileage out of that test!) and was impressed. She mentioned Marilyn to producer Hornblow and director Huston.

There the matter might have ended, with no job for Marilyn if it hadn't been for her friendships. Hyde immediately arranged for Marilyn to meet Hornblow and Huston. They thought she'd be just right for the role. Marilyn got the part but she didn't get any billing at all in a picture that was destined to be both a critical and a box-office success. But at a sneak preview in Westwood Village, the audience whooped it up whenever she appeared on the screen. Almost all the preview questionnaires filled out by the audience asked, "Who was the blonde?"

But Hollywood's bigger brains didn't get the message yet.

MGM passed her up. Her next stop was 20th Century-Fox again, where she had a small part in *All About Eve* as a dumb blonde who "is a graduate of the Copacabana School of Dramatic Art." But 20th Century-Fox didn't nail her to a contract, either. Not at first.

But one day, while Marilyn was working briefly at 20th Century-Fox, she and other stars and starlets were ordered to attend a party for exhibitors. The other stars were almost trampled in the rush of the exhibitors to get next to Marilyn. They asked her, "And what movies are *you* going to be in, Miss Monroe?" She told them sweetly, "You'll have to ask my bosses that." Spyros Skouras, the president, asked who the girl was that the exhibitors were going crazy over. They told him. Then he asked his flunkies what movies she was in. They nervously informed him that she wasn't in anything. "The exhibitors like her," he growled. "If they like her, then the public likes her. No?" The stooges hastily agreed.

Skouras was even more impressed when he found that the fan mail for this girl, who wasn't even seen on the screen—although publicity stills, saying that she was in the picture, had been widely printed—was more voluminous than the mail for any other stars on the studio's payroll. He ordered his aides to sign her to a contract. It started at $500 a week and kept rising to a ceiling of $1,500 a week. She had a couple of trivial parts, and then another friendship intervened to make her a star.

Jerry Wald was casting *Clash by Night* at RKO. Sidney Skolsky, the powerful newspaper columnist, who had been a close friend of Marilyn since her earliest days in Hollywood, suggested her for a part. RKO borrowed her from 20th Century-Fox for $3,000 for six weeks, an unbelievably cheap price. Marilyn got star billing and rave notices from the critics. She went back to 20th Century-Fox a star.

In 1952, the nude calendar burst upon the world. At first the studio thought this meant a scandal that would ruin Marilyn's usefulness. Instead, it earned her publicity she could never have obtained ordinarily. Her quick wit helped to turn the tide of public opinion. When she was asked, "Didn't you have *anything* on while the pictures were taken?" she replied blandly, "The radio."

A few weeks later she admitted that her mother was in a mental hospital, although she had previously told everyone that her mother was dead. She told how she had been contributing to her mother's support all along. Again, the disclosure won sympathy for her, not hostility.

From that point on, Marilyn's career couldn't be stopped. She was "MM," the great sex symbol.

Her personal life was less successful, and ultimately the suppressed torments—doubt, shame, fear, guilt—would destroy her professional life.

In 1950, while she was working on *All About Eve,* Marilyn saw a tall, gaunt, sad-faced man deep in conversation with Elia Kazan, the director. She asked to be introduced to the man. He was Arthur Miller, Pulitzer Prize-winning playwright (*All My Sons; Death of a Salesman*). They saw a great deal of each other during the next few weeks. Some friends of Marilyn understood that Miller was going to divorce his wife and marry her. If Marilyn thought that, she was in for heartbreak. Miller went back East to his wife.

Two years later, at a time when she was lonelier than usual, a mutual friend introduced her to baseball star Joe DiMaggio. She had never heard of him until then. In fact, when she was told he was the greatest baseball player since Babe Ruth (a claim clearly open to dispute), she asked, "Who's Babe Ruth?"

In 1954, she and Joe were married, rather abruptly, without any advance planning. At the motel in Pasa Robles where they spent their brief honeymoon, unrecognized, Joe made sure the room was equipped with television. It was a portent of things to come.

Joe couldn't stand the publicity she got, and it really bothered him when she posed publicly with her skirts above her waist for a scene in *The Seven-Year Itch,* filmed on location in New York.

On her part, she felt that Joe cared more about poker, baseball, his cronies, and TV than he did about her. Nine months after the wedding, they parted. She got a divorce, charging him with "coldness and indifference." But for the rest of her life, and even after she died, he went on loving painfully, in his own low-key, adoring way.

It was only a few months later that Arthur Miller came back into her life.

Arthur's married life had been going from bad to worse, possibly because of his memories of Marilyn and 1950. (There were many other causes, however, for the Millers' marital breakup.) In May 1955 Miller encountered Marilyn again at party in New York. She was in a simple white dress. In her hand was a drink, a screwdriver. She looked lovelier than ever.

At the time she was studying at the Actors Studio in New York, an ambitious project in which Miller had considerable interest. But Miller didn't take her home that night; actor Eli Wallach and his wife, Anne Jackson, who had taken her to the party, escorted her home. She seemed full of dreams and happy. Two weeks later Miller asked a friend for Marilyn's unlisted telephone number. All that summer and fall they met in out-of-the-way places—Long Island, Connecticut, little, obscure restaurants in New York. Usually Wallach was present, and it appeared that Marilyn was with him, not Miller. They managed to keep any hint of the affair out of the newspaper columns.

In June 1956, after she had finished work on *Bus Stop,* the story of their romance began to break in the newspapers. The press was in such hot pursuit that a girl reporter for a French magazine was killed in an auto accident trying to keep up with them.

They slipped off secretly to be married by a municipal judge in White Plains, a Westchester County suburb of New York. Two days later there was a religious ceremony: a rabbi married them in New York in a double-ring ceremony.

They had trying times ahead of them. Miller was called before a Congressional committee investigating Communism, a popular pursuit for any headline-hungry politician in those witch-hunting days. His clash with the congressmen precipitated a court fight in which Marilyn loyally upheld her husband.

At the same time, she made impossible demands on him, in the manner of insecure people: she expected him to think of nothing but her, to devote all of himself to her. His creative output dried up. He appeared to many who saw them to be little more than an aide to her, almost a flunky. Their emotional life suffered, as one might expect. Two miscarriages made matters worse. He wrote a movie for her—*The Misfits*—but then she went on to *Let's Make Love* and promptly entered into a blatant affair with Yves Montand, the French actor who was starring in it with her. In 1960, four years, three months, and thirteen days after their wedding, Arthur Miller and Marilyn Monroe separated. In January 1961 they got a Mexican divorce.

(After her death Miller wrote an autobiographical drama, *After the Fall,* which was a hit when it opened on Broadway during the 1963-64 theater season. It paints "Maggie" [Marilyn] as almost moronically stupid; "I wish I knew something," she sighs at one point. Her distrust of everyone is paranoid: "You don't see the knives people hide," she cries to "Quentin" [Miller]. Men always gravitate to her, and she finds it almost impossible to reject their advances. It is not a very kind portrait.)

Marilyn's movies had been improving, but not her temperament. *Bus Stop, How to Marry a Millionaire, Gentlemen Prefer Blondes,* and *Some Like It Hot* showed Marilyn as an actress whose technique was being steadily polished. But her personality had turned rather unpleasant. She said mean, nasty, petty, vicious things to her leading men. Don Murray, Tony Curtis, Laurence Olivier all had cause to detest her. "Vicious arrogance" and "vindictive selfishness" were some of the phrases applied to her by Curtis. She owned her own production company now, she was the queen at 20th Century-Fox, and she ruled with an iron fist. She wasn't pleasant to anyone: not the grips, not the other actors, not the production staff. She was paying everyone back for her years of humiliation and abuse.

Hers was the savagery of the unsure, the frightened, the weak. As her outward toughness was demonstrated more forcefully, her inward uncertainties began to consume her. She started to work on *Something's Got to Give* and made history of a sort by making the most famous nude swimming scene since Hedy Lamarr's in the old European film, *Ecstasy.* But she showed up on only a handful of days for work, and the costs of the film began mounting astronomically, as actors, cameramen, script persons, lighting crews, and all the others involved in film-making stood around waiting, played cards, dozed, and collected pay. It couldn't go on. The studio called off the film in the middle of production and suspended Marilyn.

She brooded, consulted her psychiatrist, saw her physician about a variety of psychosomatic disorders. She was afraid of age, of men, of inadequacy as a woman, of a possible decline in her career, of the hazards of a planned appearance on the Broadway stage, of the insanity that she feared ran in her family—above all, of loneliness.

On June 1, 1962 (her birthday), Andre de Dienes telephoned

Arthur Miller's work suffered from his marriage to Marilyn. After she'd had two miscarriages and an affair with Yves Montand, their marriage was on the rocks.
Wide World Photos

her at the Beverly Hills Hotel to wish her well. She asked him to come up and see her. She was packing for a trip to New York. She said no one else had remembered her birthday. "She was sick of lonesomeness," he said.

On August 4, according to the officials who investigated her death, she talked to Peter Lawford and asked him for the telephone number of his wife, Pat, in Hyannis Port, Massachusetts. She talked on the telephone with DiMaggio's son (by his first marriage), a Marine, about his broken engagement. She had dinner in her new home at 12305 Fifth Helena Drive, a little cul de sac in Brentwood, off Carmelina Avenue between Sunset and San Vicente Boulevards. Her dinner companion was her press agent, Pat Newcomb, and the discussion dealt with trivialities: Marilyn said she wanted to go to a movie the next day, a Sunday. Then Marilyn got another telephone call, from a caller whose identity was never established by the police—at least, it was never disclosed. That phone call appeared to upset Marilyn, or so her housekeeper,

Neither Clark Gable nor Marilyn lived to make another film after *The Misfits,* which Arthur Miller had written for the Marilyn he loved. He would draw an unkind portrait of her in *After the Fall.*

Mrs. Eunice Murray, thought. And Mrs. Murray was a good judge; she had worked with emotionally troubled people for years, as a sort of non-professional psychiatric nurse, and it was Marilyn's psychiatrist who had arranged for her to work in the house on Fifth Helena Drive.

Miss Newcomb left the house at 7 p.m. Marilyn closed and locked her door a short time later. After midnight, Mrs. Murray awoke and, walking through the house, saw the light shining under Marilyn's door. Alarmed, she tried to awaken her mistress. Then she called Marilyn's psychiatrist, who lived nearby.

Together, they broke in through a garden door of glass, and found Marilyn lying unclothed on the bed, a sheet pulled up about her head, the telephone in one hand. On her night stand were many bottles of pills (for years she had been fighting insomnia with barbiturates and then, the next morning, fighting to awake from the after-effect of grogginess by gulping amphetamines). A day or two before a doctor had given her a prescription for a strong barbiturate. That bottle was empty.

Marilyn Monroe was dead.

Almost immediately the rumors started. The mystery about the unidentified caller made the rumors inevitable, of course.

Because Marilyn was a friend of the Kennedys, many of the rumors involved them. One, for example, had her talking on the telephone to President John F. Kennedy in the White House as she was dying. When President Kennedy was assassinated in Dallas fifteen months later, on November 22, 1963, the rumors really proliferated, for now they could be printed: it is the law that a dead person cannot be libeled.

When JFK's brother, Robert F. Kennedy, was shot to death in Los Angeles on June 5, 1968, he too became fair game for the rumor mongers.

Some accounts have it that Marilyn was the mistress of Jack Kennedy; others, that Bobby Kennedy was the happy recipient of her favors; and the assertion has even been made that both of them were her lovers.

From that point it was an easy step for the right-wing political writers to conjure up a conspiracy, which is dear to the hearts of the hustlers on both fringes of the political fabric. The theory went like this: Marilyn "knew too much," as the classic cliché goes. She was threatening to cause bad publicity for the Kennedys. She had to be done away with. So the dirty deed was done—by the FBI, the CIA, assorted Kennedy relatives, friends, supporters, or goons. (The nice thing about this sort of nonsense is that one doesn't have to support any hypothesis with facts, so any ingredient can be thrown into the pot.)

Another theory is that the Kennedys didn't order the killing of Marilyn Monroe, but people who were close to them carried out the crime in the belief that they were protecting the Kennedys' interests. (That is a sort of middle-of-the-road bit of whackiness.)

Then there is the left-wing fringe element's scenario, which also includes the FBI, the CIA, or some malignant group of rightists. In his strangest—and worst—book, a biography of Marilyn, Norman Mailer states the essence of this point of view: "Political stakes were riding on her life, and even more on her death. If she could be murdered in such a way as to appear a suicide in despair at the turn of her love, what a point of pressure could be maintained afterward against the Kennedys. So one may be entitled to speak of a motive for murder. Of course, it is another matter to find that evidence exists."

Of course. But to worry about the lack of murder evidence is to quibble, or so the murder theorists generally seem to suggest.

There are two witnesses who ought to be heard on this matter.

The first is Ralph Roberts, Marilyn's masseur. Everybody, even the murder theorists, accept his testimony, as far as I know. He is on record as having said that Marilyn once asked him, during a massage, if he had heard rumors about her being romantically involved with Bobby Kennedy. Of course, Roberts replied; everybody was talking about it in Hollywood. "Well," he said she told him, "it's not true. I like him, but not physically." On the other hand, she said, she did find Jack very attractive. But there has not been a shred of evidence presented by anyone to prove that Marilyn actually had an affair with President Kennedy (although, God knows, *that* idea is not far-fetched, for Jack Kennedy was an enthusiastic womanizer).

The second witness is Dr. Ralph Greenson, Marilyn's psychiatrist. After conferring with officers of the American Psychoanalytic Association, Dr. Greenson told the *Medical Tribune* that the rumors which were being propagated about his dead patient had reached such proportions that he felt an obligation to Marilyn to clear the air by lifting one tiny corner of the veil of confidentiality. Marilyn, he said emphatically, was *not* involved romantically with any of the Kennedys. Beyond that he refused to disclose any of the matters that she confided to him during her psychotherapy.

No doubt the rumors will continue for many years, until so much time has passed that people will have to ask themselves, "Marilyn Monroe? Who's she?" She was a legend while she was alive; it is only fitting that she, and the manner of her death, should become a part of mythology when she was no longer alive.

The only thing that really counts is that a wretched little girl who had a bleak and unhappy childhood was able to cling to a dream that made her a great movie star when she grew up; but then she found that even stars need warmth, and understanding, and all the things so many of them have shed in clawing their way to the top.

The last word belongs to her first husband. On August 5, 1962, a policeman friend of James Dougherty woke him up with a telephone call at 4 a.m. to tell him what had happened. Dougherty hung up the phone, looked at his second wife, his wife of sixteen years, and said, "Say a prayer for Norma Jean. She's dead."

13 Judy, Liz, Frances, and Jayne:
The Insecurities of Stardom

Actors and actresses, on the stage, on television, or in films, more often than not are insecure people who feel a limited measure of confidence only when they hide behind the mask of a role. The men who appear on screen often harbor a feeling that there is something inherently unmanly about earning a living by acting; that is the reason so many actors show their ability to drink by consuming vast quantities of booze (proving only that any fool can be a drunk), by performing hair-raising feats on motorcycles or in cars or airplanes, or by assuming a macho attitude and sleeping with every woman who isn't protected by a stone wall. The women stars suffer similar feelings of inadequacy, but they tend to compensate, as much as possible, by sexual conquests, literal exhibitionism (including dresses that leave little or nothing to the imagination), and the kind of erratic, bizarre, arrogant, childish behavior that they believe to be the mark of an artistic temperament.

To make matters worse, "they work in an industry which exploits to the utmost their personal need for exhibitionism,

Frances Farmer's beauty came through so clearly on a screen test that Paramount signed her to a contract and brought her to Hollywood. She and Hollywood never made friends. *Freda Keefer Collection*

and at the same time views it as one of the darkest iniquities," as sociologist Hortense Powdermaker put it in her landmark study of the movie industry. "They earn more money than any other group of people in the country, but work under serf-like conditions and in a system geared to the mediocre rather than to the talented. They are regarded as property, to be bought and sold at a profit. They are pampered, flattered, and glamorized for the public, and at the same time scorned and hated by those who give the flattery and do the glamorizing. They live in luxury and have considerable power, but are treated as adolescents subject to the many controls of contract, front office, agent, business manager, publicity man.

"If proof were needed that the actors are people, it would be their deep resentment of this situation. For all members of our species, not to be regarded as human is a severe threat."

Four women stars whose lives showed the destructive effect of the "star treatment" were Frances Farmer, Elizabeth Taylor, Jayne Mansfield, and—above all—Judy Garland.

A Seattle girl, Frances Farmer developed into "a leading figure on the stage and screen in the 1930s," as the *New York Times* recalled at the time of her death in 1970.

Her family did not have money. She worked her way through the University of Washington by waiting on tables, working in a perfume factory, posing for art students, ushering in a movie theater, acting as a summer camp counselor, and serving as a singing waitress at Mount Rainier National Park. After studying journalism and dramatics, she won a newspaper subscription contest and a free trip to Moscow, which was really *terra incognita* in those days. On her return to the U.S., friends in the theater arranged for her to be given a screen test by Paramount Pictures. A woman of extraordinary beauty and rare acting ability, Miss Farmer came through so well on the test that Paramount signed her to a contract and summoned her to Hollywood.

During the next seven years she made nineteen films, starred in three Broadway plays (including the original version of Clifford Odets's *Golden Boy*), appeared in seven stock productions, played leading roles in over thirty major dramatic shows on radio, and went on personal appearances beyond count.

She had only been in Hollywood a short time when she met and married a husky, handsome fellow who had been singing

Mrs. Lillian Farmer visiting her famous daughter. Mommy had a solution when Frances disobeyed house rules in Seattle: return her to the asylum, where she had been raped by orderlies and gnawed on by rats.

Frances Farmer smirked as she was booked for 180 days in the county jail. Hollywood turned its back as the overworked actresss's breakdown escalated into a 10-year nightmare.   *Los Angeles Times Photo*

with Ted Fio Rito's dance band. His name was William Anderson, but he made what she later described as a "preposterous decision to change it to the unlikely Leif Erickson." Under that name he acted, as a standard index to films puts it, as a "second lead" for more than forty years "in unspectacular roles." Television viewers became familiar with him from 1967–69 when he reigned as the leading actor in the TV series, *High Chaparral*.

From the first, the marriage had been on shaky ground, and before long it ended in divorce. There was an intense, all-consuming affair with Odets, then the outstanding radical playwright in the U.S. (Later, when the House Un-American Activities Committee's witch-hunt was destroying lives and careers, Odets would change sides and "be in the blacklister's color guard, marching in lockstep with the worst of them," as Stefan Kanfer recalled in his book, *A Journal of the*

Plague Years.) Looking back, years afterward, Frances Farmer said the affair with Odets did much to destroy her because of the pleasure he took in alternately encouraging and humiliating her, "searing my feminine spirit . . . and degrading me in every possible manner."

That kind of emotional psychological assault she didn't need, for her mother had been tearing away at Frances's ego all her life. During the affair with Odets she began drinking heavily. It was soon apparent that she suffered from the sickness that is alcoholism.

In 1942, "a frightened, overworked, and embittered young woman," she had the first of a number of run-ins with the police for drunken driving, parole violation, and even vagrancy. Finally she had a nervous breakdown and was committed to a mental hospital. For eight years she was a patient in mental hospitals. That experience was set forth in painful detail in the book she had barely completed when she died, *Will There Really Be a Morning?*, probably the most honest and moving movie autobiography ever published. Of her years as an involuntary mental patient, she wrote:

"I passed through such unbearable terror that I deteriorated into a wild, frightened creature intent only on survival.

"And I survived.

"I was raped by orderlies, gnawed on by rats, and poisoned by tainted food.

"And I survived.

"I was chained in padded cells, strapped into straitjackets, and half drowned in ice baths.

"And I survived."

After her release, she did some acting here and there across the country, and finally found herself in Indianapolis, where a local family was able to provide the kind of emotional support, patience, and love that she had always needed and sought. There she had a television program, was named "Business Woman of the Year," made many friends, took care of stray cats. Most important of all, she underwent a profound religious experience that gave her the serenity to face the death from cancer that came to her on August 1, 1970.

Elizabeth Taylor's life has been wholly different, but it, too, reflects the abnormal pressures of Hollywood. Not long after the collapse of her first marriage (to Nicky Hilton; the union

Liz was a teen-age virgin when she married playboy Nicky Hilton. Trouble started on the honeymoon.

Wide World Photos

She married Michael Wilding when she was 20. The day after they separated Mike Todd said, "You're gonna marry me," and she did. *Wide World Photos*

lasted just 214 days), she spoke a truth that has been recalled on many occasions since:

"I have a woman's body and a child's emotions."

Hollywood did nothing to help her mature emotionally.

Born in England on February 27, 1932, to an Illinois-born art dealer and his wife, a former actress, Elizabeth Taylor was brought to the U.S. by her parents in 1939, when war broke out in Europe. Her father then took over the management of an art gallery in the Beverly Hills Hotel.

It was a heaven-sent opportunity for Liz's mother, whose own acting ambitions had been frustrated by her domestic duties. She was determined to get her daughter into motion pictures. She managed to talk Universal Pictures into signing a contract for her moppet, who was then eight years old. In *Man or Mouse* she sang a duet with Alfalfa Switzer, who was supposed to be funny. It was a picture not usually mentioned in Liz's press releases in later years, but then, anyone might be excused for wanting to forget it. When it was over, the studio decided they'd had as much of Elizabeth Taylor as they wanted. They kept paying her parents $200 a week until her year's contract was up, but they didn't bother to pick up her option.

Mrs. Taylor went looking for more work for daughter Liz.

But it was her husband who found Liz's next role. An air raid warden during World War II, he was with two other wardens one day, shortly after Pearl Harbor, when one of them, who happened to be producer Sam Marx of MGM, mentioned his search for a little girl actress who liked dogs. One thing led to another, and the next day Liz was signed to appear in *Lassie, Come Home.* She got reasonably good notices in it. Then came roles in *White Cliffs of Dover* and *Jane Eyre.* Little Liz obviously had a good start on a career in films now.

At twelve she was cast as the lead in *National Velvet,* a story about a girl's love for a horse. It was a tremendous hit and is still considered one of Hollywood's more sensitive films. It made Liz Taylor a star. At thirteen, she was earning $750 a week.

At fourteen, she discarded her schoolgirl's garb for a low-cut dress from which she threatened to burst at any moment. She already had the bust of a woman. Her measurements at that age were 37½-20-36. At fifteen, she was on the cover of *Life* and was voted by Annapolis midshipmen "The Girl We'd Abandon Ship For."

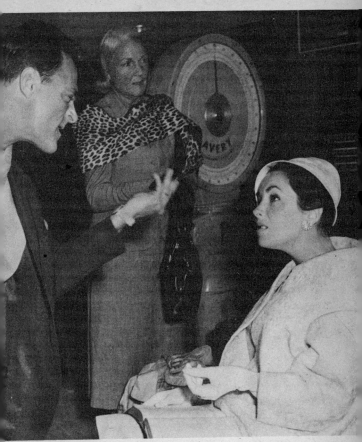

When they missed a plane at London Airport, Liz blamed Mike for being late, one word led to another, and photographers moved in. The spat ended when Mike chartered a plane to take them to Nice.

Wide World Photos

Mike and Liz and Eddie and Debbie, in 1957. Liz began
an affair with Eddie after Mike died, explaining, "Mike
is dead and I'm alive." *Wide World Photos*

At sixteen, Liz became "engaged to be engaged" to Army
Lieutenant Glenn Davis, onetime West Point football star then
in his early twenties. He went off to the Korean War. While he
was away, Liz met William Pawley, Jr., son of a rich oilman and
financier. In June 1949 their engagement was announced. By
September the engagement was off.
Then, in quick succession, the teenage movie queen dated

Howard Hughes, Roddy McDowall, Vic Damone, Montgomery Clift, baseball star Ralph Kiner.

In 1950 Liz graduated from high school. The only boy friend she invited to attend was Nicky Hilton, then the twenty-two-year-old son of hotel magnate Conrad Hilton. Three months after completing work on *Father of the Bride,* Liz married Nicky in a Catholic ceremony. Before the honeymoon was over they were having difficulties.

After the divorce Liz went to England to make the film *Ivanhoe.* On her first day in London she received a visit from Michael Wilding, whom she'd first met at MGM when she was sixteen, which was only three years earlier. He was thirty-nine then, and in the process of getting a divorce. Six days before Liz's twentieth birthday, in 1952, she married Wilding. The following year she bore him a son, Michael Howard Wilding. In 1955 a second son, Christopher Edward Wilding, was born. Sixteen months later the Wildings broke up.

The day after the separation was announced, producer Mike Todd—the glibbest, toughest, most imaginative, and brashest man in all show business (or so many people felt)—asked Liz to come to his office. There he told her, "I love you. I've been thinking about you constantly. Don't go out with anyone else. You're gonna marry me."

And she did.

He was forty-seven in 1957, and she was twenty-four, and she had been single for all of seventy-two hours when they were married in Acapulco. Cantinflas, the great Mexican comedian, was one of the witnesses.

The other witnesses were Eddie Fisher and his wife, Debbie Reynolds.

Little more than a year later, Mike Todd was killed in the crash of his private plane. He left Liz with a baby girl, Liza Todd.

In her mourning, Liz was comforted by Eddie Fisher and Debbie Reynolds, who had been very close to her and Mike. The second of the Fishers' children, Todd Emmanuel Fisher, was named for Mike.

Five months after Mike's death, Liz was in New York, stopping over on her way from Paris to Hollywood. Eddie, then thirty, went East on a business trip. He was supposed to stay four days. He stayed fourteen. And spent them with Liz.

They went to nightclubs together, took long drives out on

Long Island, and wound up by spending a very extended Labor Day weekend at Grossinger's, a popular resort in the Catskills. By that time Broadway columnist Earl Wilson, who had been carrying items hinting at a romance, broke into print with a Page One news story suggesting that the absent Debbie had lost herself a husband to the widow Todd. Other newspapers and wire services picked up the story, and soon *Time, Newsweek,* and other magazines were carrying the news.

Although Debbie and Eddie separated immediately after his belated return to Hollywood, Liz insisted she was no home-wrecker. "You can't break up a happy marriage," said she. This was hailed as profound thinking by some sloppy senti-mentalists.

When Hedda Hopper asked Liz what the not-long-dead Mike Todd would have said, Liz made a revealing comment:

"Mike is dead and I'm alive."

A storm of criticism broke over Liz Taylor's head. Columnist Elsa Maxwell summed up the feelings of Liz's critics when she said, "The facts seemed to me to prove she has been aggressive in her romances, ruthless in her disregard for the feelings of those who have stood in her path, and indifferent to the wreckage she has left behind her."

On May 12, 1959, a month and a half after she had adopted the Jewish faith, Liz married Eddie Fisher. He was filling a singing engagement in Las Vegas at the time.

From that point on, however, his career went downhill. Most of his time was spent going with his wife where her motion picture assignments led or holding her hand on the frequent occasions when she was sick. She was subject to all manner of illnesses, including periodic depressed states.

It was largely sympathy for her illnesses, in the opinion of most Hollywood people, that won her an Oscar in 1961, although the award was supposed to be for *Butterfield 8*

During the early 1960s it seemed as though journalists were vying to see who could churn out the most sickening drivel about Liz Taylor. Where once she had been, perhaps unfairly, depicted as a home-wrecking monster, she was now an angel. She was the most beautiful woman in the world (although everyone knew she'd been going to fat in recent years), the best actress (although even her most ardent admirers had to call her a "primitive" in style), the most lovable of women (although her tantrums were legendary).

Re-united after one of the separations that character-
ized their tempestuous marriages (two so far), Richard
Burton pushes Liz toward their private jet for a flight to
Naples. Her poor health has helped her image.

Wide World Photos

The truth, of course, was that Liz was neither saint nor Satan; she was a woman, the object of too much attention all her life, who was completely unequipped to cope with the ordinary challenges and restraints that civilized living imposes on us all.

That became apparent when she was making the movie *Cleopatra* in Italy. There another triangle emerged in her life, but this time Eddie Fisher was odd man out. The new man was Richard Burton, who already had a wife and kids back in London. Nevertheless, Liz got her way: the Burtons were divorced and Liz and Richard were married in 1964.

Later Fisher married singer-actress Connie Stevens, a union that ended in divorce after the birth of two daughters. In the meantime, he had the misfortune to become a patient of "Dr. Feelgood," a New York physician named Max Jacobson, whose patients included many New York, Hollywood, and Washington celebrities, drawn to him by the reports of the marvelous results he was able to achieve with injections of what his patients thought were vitamins and hormones. In fact, the injections were methamphetamine, known on the streets as "speed," and in 1975 Dr. Jacobson had his license to practice medicine taken away from him after the *New York Times* exposed the true nature of his "treatments." Speed is strongly addictive, and before Fisher kicked the habit in a Swiss hospital he was forced into bankruptcy. In 1975, after years away from show business, Fisher started to make a comeback. Looking back to his life with Liz Taylor, he still said, "Elizabeth was the only woman I really ever loved."

Clearly Richard Burton felt the same way. His marriage to Liz was a tempestuous business, with separations and fights over his drinking and over her jealousy and his. Despite all that, or perhaps even because of it, Liz won her second Oscar for the best performance she had ever achieved, playing against her husband in the 1966 film, *Who's Afraid of Virginia Woolf?* (Ironically, Burton, widely acknowledged to be one of the finest actors in the world, never won an Academy Award.)

In 1974 Liz obtained an uncontested divorce on grounds of incompatibility from a Swiss court. During the months that followed, her constant companion was Henry Wynberg, a Los Angeles used car dealer. On his part, Burton announced plans to marry Princess Elizabeth of Yugoslavia as soon as she was able to divorce her husband, a British banker. But all the time Liz and Richard were talking on the telephone at least three times a week. After fourteen months of divorce, they suddenly appeared in public together again and announced that they were planning to re-marry.

"For how long?" asked Liz's fourteen-year-old daughter, Maria Fisher Burton, whom Richard had adopted.

"Forever," Burton answered.

In Liz's life, "forever" is a matter of months.

Still another kind of Hollywood casualty was Jayne Mansfield.

Born April 19, 1933, in Bryn Mawr, Pennsylvania, she was brought up in Dallas. She was hooked on Hollywood from childhood. There wasn't a fan magazine she didn't read (and believe), and photographs of stars covered the walls of her bedroom. When she was sixteen, she found she was pregnant. She married her baby's father on May 6, 1950, and the child was born in November. Before long her husband was drafted and sent to Korea; while he was away, his wife took acting lessons in Dallas. When he came home in 1954, she

"I wanted to be a movie star since I was three," Jayne Mansfield told gaping reporters. "They told me I'd be another Shirley Temple, but I guess I outgrew it."

The Museum of Modern Art/Film Stills Archive

persuaded him to move to Hollywood. As her marriage fell apart, she kept making the rounds of the studios, looking for work.

"I've got to be a movie star," she said at the time. "I've just got to make it. I've got to be a movie star."

A small part in a television drama led to a bit role in the movie, *Female Jungle.* Then she acquired an agent and a publicity man. The latter somehow arranged for her to be included on a flying press junket to Silver Springs, Florida, for the premiere of a new Jane Russell movie, *Underwater.* Jayne sat next to the editor of *Daily Variety,* who began writing stories about her for his trade publication. At a pool party in Florida, Jayne appeared in the briefest of bikinis, showing off her dimensions, 40-18-35. "Photographs of the blonde Miss Mansfield . . . all but put Jane Russell, the star of the movie, out of sight," the *New York Times* later reported. And Jayne Mansfield wasn't even in the movie!

"I wanted to be a movie star since I was three," Jayne told the reporters. Then she added, in her best dumb-blonde fashion, "They told me I'd be another Shirley Temple, but I guess I outgrew it."

Soon newspapers and magazines were flooded with pictures of Jayne Mansfield in one publicity stunt or another. George Axelrod, the playwright, saw the pictures when he

Jayne Mansfield and her lover, Sam Brody, were killed with their driver in a car crash that decapitated Jayne (her body hurtled into the night). Her three children, in the back seat, were unharmed.   *Wide World Photos*

was casting his new Broadway comedy, *Will Success Spoil Rock Hunter?* A satire of the movie industry, the play opened with Jayne, wrapped inadequately in a towel, lying on a massage table. The critics generally agreed that Jayne's playing was largely responsible for the play's run of 452 performances. The associate producer, Sylvia Herscher, was later quoted as saying, "She didn't act the role; she *was* the role."

Returning to Hollywood in triumph, she continued to ride a wave of publicity, but now she was getting some worthwhile roles. Her best acting was in the part of a wistful derelict in the 1957 movie of John Steinbeck's *The Wayward Bus.*

Divorced from her first husband, she married Mickey Hargitay, a former Mr. Universe, in 1958. The muscle man had been part of Mae West's act when Jayne met him, and their fight over him made comic headlines for a time. The Hargitay marriage ended in divorce and there was a third marriage in 1964, but that lasted only two years.

Through it all, Jayne engaged in sex with a lack of inhibition that was breathtaking. As her biographer, Martha Saxton (*Jayne Mansfield and the American Fifties),* said, "[Her agent] feels that she never understood that sex and business were separate. When one of her advisers did something successful for her, she would often offer sex as a reward."

"She was so vulnerable and terribly insecure," said one of the men in her life, Greg Bautzer.

Although she made a number of pictures, none of them amounted to much, and there was a general sense that her career was in a decline. She was drinking more, too; her diet was reported to be one cup of beef bouillon, one bottle of bourbon, and one bottle of champagne a day.

She was also immersing herself in diabolism. Always interested in the occult, she attended a small occult discussion group in the early 1960s, and stayed with it as it grew into the Church of Satan, headed by Anton La Vey. In his book on the occult, Francis King wrote:

"I am told that [Jayne] . . . always tried to attend the regular Friday night meetings at which the altar was the body of a naked woman—I suspect that the main attraction of the Church [of Satan] for Jayne was its ultra-permissive sexual morality."

Plagued with law suits and personal problems, Jayne went to Biloxi, Mississippi in June 1967 to appear in a supper club.

With her she took three of her children and Sam Brody, her lawyer and, for the moment, her principal lover. On June 28 the five of them left by car for New Orleans, eighty miles away where Jayne was scheduled to be on a television talk show in the morning. A nineteen-year-old driver for the supper club was in the front, Jayne was on the passenger's side, and Brody was in the middle. The three children and the baggage were in the back seat.

The car was going fast, but the supper club's driver began to slow down when he saw what appeared to be fog ahead of him on Route 90. In fact, a mosquito-spraying machine, heavy and slow-moving, was laying down a cloud of insecticide. Although he was slowing down, the driver of the Mansfield car was still going at a fair rate of speed when he drove into the cloud.

At 2:25 on the morning of June 29, the Mansfield Buick smashed into the spraying truck. Most of the car was rammed under the truck, the top of the car being ripped off by the force of the impact. The three kids, thrown to the floor in back, escaped major injury. The driver and Brody were hurled away from the wreck and killed. Jayne Mansfield was decapitated before her body, too, went hurtling through the night.

The girl who had grown up on dreams of Hollywood met death far from Hollywood and Vine. Her movie career, such as it was, had spanned some ten years.

But the quintessential victim of the fantasy that is Hollywood was Judy Garland.

Born Frances Ethel Gumm, in Grand Rapids, Minnesota, on June 10, 1922, she was an unwanted child. There were already two other children, it had been five years since the last baby was born, and neither parent wanted the burden of another child. But the medical student they approached about an abortion rejected their appeal, so the baby was born.

She would often, during her brief lifetime, find herself wishing she had never been born; and there were others, victimized by her preoccupation with self, her tantrums, her eccentricities, who would also wish it.

Her father ran the local theater. Her mother played the piano there. While she was still a baby she was encouraged to sing before audiences; her first stage appearance was at the age of two, which is the sort of thing no paying audience should be forced to put up with. She was not yet into her teens

Judy and husband Vincente Minnelli on the set of *Meet Me in St. Louis.* "Mama was just like a beautiful flower that withered and died," said daughter Liza.

The Museum of Modern Art/Film Stills Archive

when she began to resent the fact that her parents were given to "winding me up to sing, and then putting me back in the closet when they were finished with me."

As the baby of the family, and a truly attractive child, Frances was spoiled. If she wanted to buy candy or ice cream, she could just take the money, even if the family couldn't afford it. She was permitted to win card games by cheating. Although her sisters were spanked and sometimes sent to bed

At 46, Judy married Mickey Deans, a 35-year-old discotheque manager. Three months later the M.G.M. star who had kept going on "uppers" and "downers" for years was dead from an overdose of sleeping pills.

Wide World Photos

without dinner, her father once justified his failure to discipline Frances by saying that discipline was "a word that belongs in the dictionary. We don't use it around here." All little Frances had to do to get what she wanted was throw a tantrum.

So she grew up without any guidelines to help her develop patterns of socially acceptable behavior. Because she was permitted to cheat to win, she never learned how to lose. Never having lost a point, and never having been deprived of what she wanted, she never learned how to cope with disappointment.

For the sake of her health, and in the hope of making more money running a theater, the family moved to Lancaster, California, north of Los Angeles on the edge of the Mojave Desert. But it was not in Southern California that the first professional breakthrough occurred; that happened in Chicago, where their mother had taken the three Gumm sisters to entertain at the 1934 World's Fair, the theme of which was "A Century of Progress."

The group got a chance to fill in for a missing vaudeville act at the Oriental Theater. George Jessel was master of ceremonies, and he was so impressed with the singing of Frances that he arranged for the William Morris talent agency to represent them. He also selected a new name for the group—the Garland Sisters, preferable to their real name because audiences always laughed at *that*. (Garland was the name of the theater critic of the now defunct *New York World Telegram*.)

When they returned to Los Angeles, Jessel arranged, through his friend, Billy Wilkerson, publisher of the *Hollywood Reporter* (the same man who "discovered" Lana Turner and who was a partner with Bugsy Siegel in the Flamingo at Las Vegas), for the Garlands to get a tryout at the Trocadero, a restaurant on Sunset Strip. The show business journal, *Variety*, caught the act, thought well of it generally, but raved about Frances Garland as a show-stopper. "Class entertainment," *Variety* said, "Possessing a voice that, without a P.A. system, is audible throughout a house as large as the Chinese, she handles ballads like a veteran and gets every note and word over with a personality that hits audiences."

Over the next few months, the Garland sisters filled a number of singing engagements. One was at the Cal-Neva Lodge at Lake Tahoe, on the California-Nevada border. There

Frances took a new first name from the title of Hoagy Carmichael's new hit, "Judy." Now Frances Gumm had been turned into Judy Garland.

While she and her sisters were at the Cal-Neva, some studio people heard Judy sing. One of them told Louis B. Mayer that he had to audition this girl. Several others who had heard her had been telling him the same thing, so he finally gave in and consented to listen to her sing. Then he understood why so many people who didn't even know this kid were such enthusiastic boosters for her. On October 1, 1935, she was signed to an MGM contract.

In the years that followed, she made more than thirty-five motion pictures (including the "Andy Hardy" series, *The Wizard of Oz, Babes in Arms, Strike Up the Band, Ziegfeld Girl, For Me and My Gal, Girl Crazy, Meet Me in St. Louis, Ziegfeld Follies,* and *A Star Is Born*), set a New York vaudeville record with an engagement of nineteen weeks and 184 performances, cut a great many records, and, toward the end of her life, made a number of television appearances. An instinctive actress, an inspired comedienne, she had a singing voice that was full and sweet, with just an edge of brassiness to it. And she had a talent—as very few performers have ever displayed—to win over an audience so completely that it became almost fanatically devoted to her. As one critic said, a typical Garland appearance was "more than a concert—it was a tribal celebration." Audiences would often shout before, during, and after her performance, "We love you, Judy!"

When the bad times came, and the drugs and the alcohol and the nerves and the abuse of her body had taken its toll and her voice was almost completely gone, her fans would still cheer and applaud her wildly, and many would weep unashamedly.

For the bad times did come. It was fated. Her parents had spoiled her and taught her self-indulgence and egocentricity and MGM, anxious to keep a valuable "property" contented, followed the same policy. "She therefore never had a chance to acquire the quality that could have sustained her talent over the years," as one of her obituaries put it.

The pressure, and the lack of support that discipline might have provided, began to take its toll at an early age. When she was eighteen and making $150,000 a picture, she was already under a psychiatrist's care.

That was only to be expected. A year earlier, the pressure had intensified when she won a special Oscar for her work in *The Wizard of Oz,* in which she sang, among other tunes, "Over the Rainbow," the song that became her trademark. But how could anyone keep up that pace? At seventeen, an Academy Award; where could she go but down? She had already reached the peak.

As one might expect, her emotional problems became obvious in her personal life before her performances were affected. On July 28, 1941, she married composer and orchestra leader David Rose; they were divorced three years later. In 1945 she married director Vincente Minnelli; their marriage resulted in the birth of one child, Liza, but ended in divorce in March 1952. Next came Sid Luft, onetime test pilot, a producer of undistinguished films, and the ex-husband of actress Lynn Bari; two children were born to that union, Lorna and Joseph. Judy's marriage to Luft ended in divorce in 1965. A few weeks later she married Mark Herron, only to divorce him two years later. Her last husband was Mickey Deans, 35, a discotheque manager whom she wed in 1969.

Three months after her fifth wedding, Deans answered a transatlantic telephone call from two of Judy's friends. They wanted to talk to her; although it was 2 a.m. in Los Angeles, it was 10 a.m. in London. The call had awakened Deans from a sound sleep, and he said Judy wasn't in bed, she must be in the bathroom. He went to get her. A few minutes later he was back on the phone.

"Judy's dead," he said, almost hysterically.

The date was June 22, 1969.

During the last few years of her life, her emotional state had bordered on chaos. She would arrive very late on the set for motion pictures. During concert appearances on stage, she might sing long past the scheduled time; on the other hand, she might refuse to perform at all. Her voice, affected by the "uppers" and "downers" she had been taking for years, was a pathetic caricature of the bell-like voice she had projected early in her career. Although Sid Luft helped her with her business affairs and other matters long after their divorce—to the day of her death, in fact—she sometimes turned on him with paranoid suspicion and hostility. Even her children were sometimes the target of her confused animosity.

She had attempted suicide several times during her life, but the English coroner, after carefully considering all the evidence, decided there was no evidence that she had taken her own life. It appeared, he said, that Judy Garland had died from an "incautious overdosage" of sleeping pills. The coroner theorized that she had taken enough sleeping pills upon retiring so that she was in a groggy state when she awoke in the middle of the night. Too drugged already to realize how many pills she had taken, she had proceeded to take more— many more—"more barbiturates than her body could tolerate."

When the novel, *Valley of the Dolls,* was being turned into a movie many in Hollywood believed that the character of "Neely" was based on Judy Garland. Judy was asked to play the part of "Helen Lawson." That deal fell through, but it is of some interest that the story dealt with people in show business who got by from day to day on "uppers" and "downers."

An almost unknown actress would play one of the major roles in that film. Her name was Sharon Tate, and her name would be on all the front pages before long.

14 Bruce Lee and James Dean:
How Cults Are Born

On July 20, 1973, a Chinese actor named Bruce Lee died in Hong Kong at the age of thirty-two. Although such an event would certainly call for an autopsy in any part of the developed world, one might think the death otherwise of little interest to anyone. One might be wrong.

For Bruce Lee's motion pictures, popular during his lifetime, became even more popular after his death, and there was every sign that his death was being used as the basis for a new cult, just as the violent death of James Dean in 1955 had resulted in the creation of an astonishing cult.

Although the critics were virtually unanimous in panning Lee's motion pictures, they were astonishing commercial successes. Because Lee made a career of karate, kung-fu, and other martial arts, they always contained a scene in which Lee (always the Guy in the White Hat) confronted the principal villains and overcame them simply by application of his arsenal of personal weapons: fists, the edge of the hand, the feet, and any other useful part of the body.

Among his motion pictures was a movie called variously *The Big Boss* and *Fist of Fury*. Vincent Canby, the movie critic,

said in the *New York Times* that movies like *Fist of Fury* make
"the worst Italian Western look like the most solemn and
noble achievements of the early Soviet cinema."

Lee was born in San Francisco, and studied philosophy at
the University of Washington. He also appeared on television
in "Batman" and as "Cato," the chauffeur, in "The Green
Hornet." But it was with his kung-fu films, made in Hong
Kong, that he achieved his greatest popularity.

After his death the process of immortalizing him, of bringing
him back to life, began, as it had with another actor, James
Dean, twenty years earlier. A recent book on Lee, for example, reported that "there is a tribe in Malaysia which believes
Bruce Lee is still alive and his reported death on July 20, 1973,
was merely a publicity stunt for a film he was working on then,
The Game of Death."

That's the beginning, the planting of the seed.

In fact, Lee (the family name was originally Li) appeared not
to take himself nearly as seriously as his fans did. He once told
Black Belt magazine, "People ask me as an actor, 'How good
are you really in kung-fu?' I always kid them about that. If I tell
them I'm good, they'll probably say I'm boasting, but if I tell
them I'm no good, I'm lying. I tell them to believe half of what
they see and nothing that they hear—and remember, 700
million Chinese can't be all Wong."

Lee's popularity cut across racial, ethnic, cultural, and
economic lines. When Tatum O'Neal, the ten-year-old star of
Paper Moon, was asked to name her favorite movie, she
responded at once: "*Five Fingers of Death,*" a Bruce Lee
opus. Obviously, Bruce Lee was a very special phenomenon,
the sort of person whose life, and death, tend to give rise to
legends.

On the afternoon of his death, Lee complained of a head-
ache. Betty Ting-pei, an associate, offered him a prescription
pain killer, Equagesic. For several hours afterward he seemed
perfectly normal. In fact, he took a nap, and, according to one
of his aides, was "sleeping peacefully."

But too soundly. When a friend, Raymond Chow, tried to
awaken the sleeping man, he couldn't. He testified at the
inquest that he tried to wake the man up by slapping his face,
but there was no response. The inquest took note of the fact
that in his films Lee had often received blows that weren't
included in the scripts. Some of those blows had been quite
severe.

Bruce Lee, the Chinese-American king of celluloid kung-fu, died at 32 of peculiar causes which gave rise to wild and various speculation.

The laboratory analysis of the contents of his digestive system showed traces of cannabis (marijuana) in Lee's stomach. But marijuana does not kill.

The clinical pathologist who testified at the inquest said he thought Lee had died because of a hypersensitive reaction to Equagesic or to some other substances. He also disclosed that Lee had suffered for a long time from a convulsive disorder which compelled him to take pills three times a day. Nevertheless, the family insisted that he did not have epilepsy

There the inquest ended, and the rumors began. Lee had been killed by rivals. An herb well known in the Far East but unheard of in our country was used to poison him. He had a lot of enemies, and one of them put out a contract on him.

That's only the beginning. We may expect to hear a great deal more about Bruce Lee and his demise in the months and years ahead.

As we did with James Dean.

James Dean—his middle name was Byron—only made three pictures during his brief lifetime, but they were all big ones: *East of Eden,* in 1954; *Rebel Without a Cause* in 1955; and *Giant,* in 1955. Before *Giant* was released he was dead. He was cast in his first film cast as a moody, restless son; *Rebel Without a Cause* further identified him with youth at a time when the first rumblings of turbulence and disorder were being perceived, dimly, by a few people.

Five years after Dean left his uncle's Indiana farm, in 1949 at the age of eighteen, he was a famous film star. In 1955 he was buried in a small cemetery just north of Fairmount, a small farming community.

Or so the official story goes.

I believe that story. A lot of cultists don't.

For example, in 1973 several publications, including a rag called the *National Examiner,* blossomed out—if that's the word—with headlines like this: "James Dean Did Not Die in 'Fatal' Auto Accident. Paralyzed and Mutilated, He's Hidden in a Sanatorium."

Dean's mother died when he was a small boy. His father moved to the West Coast and remarried, leaving his son to be raised by relatives. After graduating from high school, young Dean joined his father in West Los Angeles while he went to Santa Monica City College. A part in a television drama brought him to the attention of the movie industry.

One night he was swinging at a gay party, the next day he was gone. "He had an idée fixe about me," said Marlon Brando.

News reached the James Dean Memorial Foundation that the bronze head atop Dean's memorial column had disappeared from the cemetery.   *Wide World Photos*

About 1955 he bought a little silver Porsche Spyder, an automobile designed for racing. On Thursday, September 29, 1955, he felt good. He was planning to take the new car out for a real test the next day.

That evening he went to a "gay" party at Malibu Colony. Although he may have had bisexual tendencies, Dean was definitely homosexual,—and he tended to mix with homosexuals whose specialty was for sadism and masochism. At the party, Dean had a bad row with one of his lovers, who attacked him for feigning an interest in women.

The following morning he set out for Salinas, about 300 miles north of Los Angeles, to take part in a road race that was scheduled to be held there. In order to check out the engine, master mechanic Rolf Wuetherich rode with him toward Salinas. After driving for a couple of hours, they stopped for a snack. A short time later, Dean and Wuetherich found themselves picking up speed down Route 99 out of the mountains on to the plain south of Bakersfield. The incline was called Grapevine Grade. A policeman spotted the Porsche, saw it was going too fast, chased it, and gave Dean a summons for doing 65 m.p.h. in a 45-mile zone.

Turning left on to Route 46 north of Bakersfield, Dean and Wuetherich found themselves on a narrow, two-way road. At Blackwell's Corners Dean stopped to admire a gray Mercedes parked in front of the restaurant and store. The owner came out while he was going over the car. It seemed that the Mercedes belonged to Lance Reventlow, then twenty-one, the son of dime-store heiress Barbara Hutton. Reventlow was planning to enter the race the next day, too.

Again they took to the road, which now began to undulate with the gently rolling countryside. Down a slope they went toward a valley at the bottom. Another car, black and white, rounded a curve down there and started to climb toward them. Dean's Porsche was doing 85 on the down grade.

Suddenly the wheels of the oncoming black and white car crossed the line into their lane. The car was bearing down on them. A head-on collision seemed imminent.

"That guy's got to stop!" Dean cried.

But the car didn't stop.

With a deafening, grinding crunch, the two cars crashed.

James Dean was dead. Wuetherich suffered a broken jaw, a fractured leg, and multiple contusions and abrasions. The driver of the car that plowed into them walked away from the wreck with a bruised nose and a bloody forehead.

The funeral services were barely over when the James Dean cult began to develop—a cult that is flourishing to this day. Just think: in the past eighteen months two books (at least) have been published about a movie star who died twenty years ago and only made three pictures.

Fan magazines continued to publish articles about Dean. Serious journals of the cinema carried analytical essays. There were James Dean records and tapes, James Dean souvenirs (busts, masks, knives, rings). Hundreds of fan clubs sprang into existence all over the world.

Two or three years after Dean's death, Marlon Brando told Truman Capote, who was writing a profile for the *New Yorker*, "I hardly knew him. But he had an *idée fixe* about me. Whatever I did, he did. . . . When I finally met Dean . . . it was at a party where he was throwing himself around, acting like a madman. So I spoke to him. I took him aside and asked him didn't he know he was sick. That he needed help. . . . He listened to me. He knew he was sick [emotionally]. I gave him the name of an analyst and he went. And at least his work improved. Toward the end I think he was beginning to find his own way as an actor. . . .

"This glorifying of Dean is all wrong. . . . He wasn't a hero. . . . He really was—just a lost boy trying to find himself."

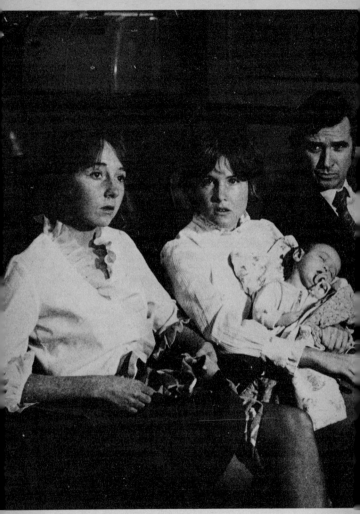

Sandra Goode Pugh and Lynette "Squeaky" Fromme
listened as Manson was accused of car theft. Later
Squeaky made history when she tried to assassinate
President Ford.   *United Press International Photo*

15 Sharon Tate:
Sex, Satanism, and Sacrifice

It is rare that a Hollywood occurrence, no matter how spectacular, reaches out to touch the U.S. Presidency directly. Even the death of Marilyn Monroe only tangentially affected the Presidency, because of questions raised about her relationship with the Kennedys. But the murder of Sharon Tate and her friends almost changed the course of history on September 5, 1975, when Lynette Alice (Squeaky) Fromme, a follower of Charles Manson, who was in prison for the Tate slayings, almost killed President Gerald Ford. From that moment on, there could be no question that the Sharon Tate case was one of the strangest and most extraordinary episodes ever recorded in the history of Hollywood or, indeed, in all of U.S. history.

As far as the public was concerned, it began shortly after 8 a.m. on August 9, 1969, when a middle-aged black woman, Mrs. Winifred Chapman, who was the housekeeper of a home at 10050 Cielo Drive, a secluded street that pushes up a draw off Benedict Canyon Drive in Los Angeles, arrived for work and found five persons had been butchered there during the night. Screaming, the unfortunate woman ran down the driveway to the other houses on Cielo to give the alarm.

"Murder——death——bodies——blood!" she screamed.

Someone heard her, and soon the area was swarming with policemen and newspaper reporters.

The most notable of the five was Sharon Tate, an actress who had played a major role in *Valley of the Dolls.* Eight months pregnant, she was the wife of Roman Polanski, director of *Rosemary's Baby* and many another bizarre and macabre motion picture.

The murders were soon solved, but the case has raised questions about some of the strange cults that exist out of sight in America and in Europe, including sects that worship the devil. Other questions persist about possible prior encounters between some of the victims and various members of the Manson family.

To put these matters into perspective, it is necessary to briefly recapitulate the Sharon Tate murders, and other slayings related to them.

The estate on Cielo Drive was owned by Rudi Altobelli, who

Sharon Tate and Roman Polanski in *The Fearless Vampire Killers.* Polanski, who was away when his wife was murdered, also directed a film about devil worship, *Rosemary's Baby.*

The Museum of Modern Art/Film Stills Archive

Charles Manson clowned for photographers after the judge ordered him out of court. Who was whose puppet?   *United Press International Photo*

was business manager for several show business celebrities. It had been occupied by actress Doris Day's son, Terry Melcher, a television and record producer, who had lived there with actress Candice Bergen, the daughter of ventriloquist Edgar Bergen. But he had moved out to his mother's house at Malibu. Later the Polanskis had rented the house, moving in on February 15, 1969.

At the time of the murders, Polanski was working in Europe. His wife was at the house, preparing for the birth of their child. The others who were killed along with her were:

Jay Sebring, thirty-five, who owned hair styling salons in Hollywood, San Francisco, New York, and London. He had once been engaged to Sharon, but she had broken the engagement after meeting Polanski. Sebring, who lived in the house at 9860 Easton Drive where Jean Harlow's husband died, had been stabbed seven times and shot once.

Abigail Folger, daughter of the chairman of the board of the A.J. Folger Coffee Company, a Procter and Gamble subsidiary. She was twenty-five years old. She was stabbed twenty-eight times.

Voytek Frykowski, thirty-two, who had known Polanski in Poland. After leaving his homeland in 1967, he had been introduced to Abby Folger by the emigre Polish novelist Jerzy Kosinski. They had become lovers, and he had been living off her fortune. The killers had shot him twice, beaten him over the head thirteen times, and plunged knives into him fifty-one times.

Steven Parent, eighteen, who didn't even know the other victims, had been visiting the caretaker of the property, William Garretson, nineteen, who was living in the guesthouse sixty feet away from the main house and screened from it by trees. Parent was slain in his car, near the gate as he was leaving the estate. Garretson was in the guesthouse during the entire massacre, but police subsequently determined that he had been unaware of what was happening at the main house because the music on his stereo prevented him from hearing the screams.

"How come I wasn't murdered?" Garretson asked the police.

They had no answer for him.

On the evening of the following day, Sunday, August 10, Leno LaBianca, forty-four, the owner of a chain of super markets, and his wife, Rosemary, thirty-eight, were found murdered in their home at 3301 Waverly Drive, in the Los Feliz district of Los Angeles. Like the victims on Cielo Drive, they had been slain with a ferocity that veteran detectives had never seen before.

The story of the Tate-LaBianca murders, as they came to be called, has been told at length in two excellent books: *The Family,* by Ed Sanders, who was a reporter for the *Los Angeles Free Press,* focuses on the killers and their milieu; *Helter Skelter,* by Vincent Bugliosi with Curt Gentry, tells the story from the point of view of those who tried to identify, track down, and convict them, for Bugliosi was the prosecutor in the case. There is no reason to repeat the details of the hunt here. It is sufficient to say that, despite almost incredible police bungling—set forth in indignant detail by Bugliosi—it was finally discovered that Charles Manson, a dirty, scruffy ex-convict and sometime pimp, had been committing murders and many other crimes with the help of what he called his "family," an aggregation of men and women, most of the latter in their teens or early twenties, who lived a communal life based on drugs and indiscriminate sex.

Manson and three of his devoted followers—Patricia Krenwinkel, Susan Atkins, and Leslie Van Houten—were found guilty in the Tate-LaBianca murders. The motive for the killings was mind boggling. Manson, it was learned, believed that the blacks would be suspected of perpetrating the massacres. The outrage in the white community would be such that a race war would explode that would end in a black victory. Manson the racist assumed that the blacks would naturally be incapable of ruling and, somehow recognizing Charlie Manson's leadership qualities, would bestow upon him the mantle of power.

Four other men who were part of the Manson "family" were convicted in other killings. They were Robert Beausoleil, Charles Watson, Steve Grogan, and Bruce Davis.

That didn't clear up all of the group's crimes. Manson had boasted of having been responsible for thirty-five killings, and not all of the victims were discovered. Moreover, some authorities believed that the actual number of victims might number one hundred or more.

And the murders continued. In 1972 two of the Manson girls and two members of a prison-born organization called the Aryan Brotherhood were arrested for the murder of a young couple, James and Lauren Willett. Squeaky Fromme, who would later aim a loaded .45 caliber automatic at President Ford from a distance of two feet in Sacramento to protest Manson's imprisonments, also was arrested in the Willetts' slaying, but the charges against her were later dropped for lack of evidence.

Obviously, the problem of the Manson "family" did not end with the convictions in the Tate-LaBianca case. Nor did many of the questions about curious coincidences in the Sharon Tate case find answers. Instead, the questions seemed to multiply as time went on.

To examine those questions, we must go back to the massacre on Cielo Drive.

Sharon Tate was a beautiful child who grew into a beautiful woman. When she was six months old she was Miss Tiny Tot of Dallas. The daughter of a career Army officer, she moved from place to place frequently with her family, collecting new beauty titles almost everywhere: at sixteen, "Miss Richland, Washington"; at seventeen, "Miss Autorama"; in the Vicenza American High School at Verona, Italy, Homecoming Queen and Queen of the Senior Prom.

In 1963 she went to Hollywood, acquired an agent, won roles in a few commercials, and then auditioned for the TV series, "Petticoat Junction." Producer Martin Ransohoff, the head of Filmways, Inc., saw her on the set and promised to make her a star—or so the story went. Certainly he lavished a lot of attention on her during the next few years. She took lessons in singing, acting, and dancing. Occasionally she appeared on television in "Petticoat Junction" and "The Beverly Hillbillies." She had small parts in two movies, *The Americanization of Emily* and *The Sandpiper*.

She appeared in a French film, *13* (also called *Eye of the Devil*), the story of a devil-worshipping cult which engages in human sacrifice. She "portrayed a chillingly beautiful but expressionless girl engaged in witchcraft," as the *New York Times* reported.

In her next film, *Don't Make Waves,* she was also deadpan, this time as a skydiver.

The common denominator of all her performances seemed to be the lack of expression on her face. Even as "Jennifer" in *Valley of the Dolls,* her most important role, she was impassive.

Her inscrutability apparently was matched by a certain passivity, at least until she met Polanski. Bugliosi says that "she seemed attracted to dominant men"; in fact, she appears to have had some strong masochistic tendencies. Bugliosi tells of a French actor with whom she had a long affair; the man once beat her so badly that she required hospital treatment.

Jay Sebring, who had been her lover for quite a while before she met Polanski, had sadistic tastes that must have surfaced during their relationship. According to an official report during the investigation, "He was considered a ladies' man and took numerous women to his residence in the Hollywood hills. He would tie the women up with a small sash cord and, if they agreed, would whip them, after which they would have sexual relations."

Drugs also figured in the case, to some extent, although they were not a major factor. Marijuana and hashish were found in various places in the house and in a sports car owned by Sebring, but they could have been found in thousands of other houses in California and in tens of thousands of places throughout the country. But a gram of cocaine was also found in Sebring's car, and in the bedroom used by Folger and Frykowski were ten capsules of a drug called MDA.

According to the Los Angeles Police Department, Sebring "used drugs as a habit." So did Abby Folger and Frykowski. They knew dope dealers across the country and narcotics dealers often visited them at the Cielo Drive house. Abby "always seemed to be in a stupor from narcotics," according to one friend of the Polanskis. As for her lover, a police report on Frykowski said, "He used cocaine, mescaline, LSD, marijuana, hashish in large amounts. . . . He was an introvert and gave invitations to almost everyone he met to come visit him at his residence. Narcotic parties were the order of the day."

Whether the sex life on Cielo Drive was out of the ordinary isn't quite clear. According to Bugliosi, police found a can of videotape showing Sharon Tate and Roman Polanski making love, but that isn't necessarily significant. Indeed, considering Polanski's unrestrained admiration for himself, it may have simply reflected a certain narcissism on his part. "Who shall I gratify tonight?" Polanski used to say, before his marriage to Sharon.

The weirdest aspect of the Sharon Tate case is the way witchcraft, devil-worship, and sexual magic cults keep entering the picture. Manson said that he was drawn to an interest in the occult while he was in prison, where he met some devil-worshippers. At his request, friends began mailing him books on the black arts. After his release from prison on March 21, 1967, Manson began assembling his "family" and he also made contact with a cult called the Devil's Disciples, in Mendocino County. From then on Manson was constantly involved with various groups engaged in satanism, witchcraft, and magical rites involving sexual acts of all kinds. His deepest involvement was with the cult that called itself the Church of the Final Judgment; it was usually referred to by its adherents simply as "The Process."

One of Manson's most fanatical followers, Susan Atkins, who personally plunged a knife into some of his victims, was deep into satanism before she met Manson. "She became involved with Anton La Vey, the Satanist," according to a court psychiatric report. La Vey, founder of the First Church of Satan in San Francisco, is the same satanist whose name popped up in connection with Jayne Mansfield. La Vey served as a technical consultant to Roman Polanski during the filming of *Rosemary's Baby,* and he also played the part of the Devil in that movie—one of a number of coincidences in the case.

There were other direct connections between satanism and the Manson group. For example, Patricia Krenwinkel, a Manson disciple convicted of murder, doodled Devil's heads and the "Mendes Goat," a devil-worship symbol, during her trial. And Charles (Tex) Watson, on the point of plunging a knife into Frykowski's body, told his victim, "I am the Devil and I'm here to do the Devil's business."

Then there is the puzzling matter of Robert Beausoleil, who was convicted of committing one of the Manson "family" murders, the torture slaying of musician Gary Hinman, who was put to death over a period of two days in his house on Old Topanga Road in Malibu. In 1967 Beausoleil was in San Francisco, living, according to Ed Sanders, with Kenneth Anger, "who introduced him to the universe of magic, not to mention the cruelty-streaked universe of Aleister Crowley," the late English poet who also wrote books on the occult and became legendary for his celebrations of the Black Mass.

Anger was a middle-aged underground film-maker whose pictures dealt primarily with homosexuality, sadism and masochism, and satanism. Ronald Tavel, another underground screenwriter and playwright, has said that Anger was "sin-

Robert Kenneth Beausoleil after being sentenced to the gas chamber. Like Kenneth Anger, he was involved in satanism.

United Press International Photo

Cappy, Kathy, Mary, Sandra Goode, and Brenda *(clockwise from upper left)* maintained a constant vigil outside the Hall of Justice.

United Press International Photo

gularly aptly-named" because his work "conveys a distrust of human beings so overwhelming that the life of the entire race is defined as little more than a sadomasochistic orgy." British film critic Roy Armes said Anger was outspoken about "his belief in the validity of Aleister Crowley's magic."

Francis King, who published a study of sexuality and magic, expressed the belief that Anger was probably responsible for similarities between the principles of Aleister Crowley and the Church of Satan, which was incorporated in San Francisco on April 30, 1966, a year before Manson's release from prison. Apparently there was some degree of involvement by Anger in the Church of Satan—the organization of La Vey, Polanski's adviser on *Rosemary's Baby.*

Beausoleil lived with Anger for some time and performed in the title role of one of Anger's films, *Lucifer Rising.* During that time Beausoleil was actively associated with a satanist group called the Companions of Life, or the Church of Final Judgment. That latter name was often used by Manson as time went on. After Squeaky Fromme's arrest for attempting to kill the President, her Manson "family" associate, Sandra Good, warned that "the Church of Final Judgment" had a list of hundreds of leading persons who were to be put to death. With scores of Manson followers and allies scattered across the U.S. and Canada, nobody felt inclined to scoff at the threat.

Finally, Alex Saunders, a life-long disciple of Aleister Crowley and a technical adviser during the filming of one of Sharon Tate's films, *13* [*Eye of the Devil*], has been quoted as claiming that he initiated Sharon Tate into witchcraft during that production. It was said that Saunders had photos showing Sharon standing within a magic circle during a satanist ritual.

Completing the coincidences are the films of Sharon Tate and Roman Polanski. The first and only movie which she ever made for him was *The Fearless Vampire Killers, or Pardon Me, But Your Teeth Are in My Neck,* a spoof of horror films. Polanski has said that he is not interested in the supernatural but every critic has expressed curiosity about Polanski's apparent preference for making motion pictures that deal with witchcraft and death. Besides *Rosemary's Baby,* there was *Cul de Sac,* showing the futility of struggle against a terrible menace, and *Do You Like Women?,* about cannibals who dine on pretty young women.

Witchcraft, sex, and violence—they run like tangled threads all through the Tate murders. Even after Manson's conviction, his group's correspondence with him, according to the associate warden at Folsom prison, "dealt with the occult." When Fromme and Good met with reporters, they wore red robes— "red with sacrifice, the blood of the sacrifice."

Even reporters and official investigators assigned to find out more about the activities of the cult became so frightened that they kept refusing to follow the trail of sadistic crime, especially after being threatened by empty-eyed, zombie-like disciples who said, like Squeaky Fromme, "We respond with our knives."

Throughout the Manson investigations and trials, everybody who came into contact with his followers talked about how they appeared to have been "programmed" by some complex psychological process. But Anger, in a book on Hollywood that devoted just two sentences to the Sharon Tate case, referred to Manson as a "programmed puppet." It had generally been assumed that the Manson followers were his "puppets," programmed by him to kill on command. But could it be that Manson, too, was just a "puppet," programmed to fill his own role in the deadly scheme of things? In that case, who programmed Charles Manson?

The questions are only succeeded by more questions, and here is the uneasy sense that loathsome, evil, merciless forces are stirring beneath the surface of society, that the Manson family may have represented simply the first of many manifestations of a tendency of the crazies to gather together for a coordinated assault against the bastions of sanity and human compassion.

In several Western states, authorities report several hundred cattle killed in a strange way. The blood of the animals had been drained, as though by cultists who might drink it in their rituals. Tails, sex organs, lips, one eye, ears, tongues, udders, and often rectums were removed and taken away, along with strips of facial and belly hide. In El Paso County, Colorado, Undersheriff Garry Gibbs expressed the fright and suspicion of many ranchers when asked about the identity of the perpetrators:

"Devil worshippers."

That was the legacy of the Sharon Tate murders: suspicion, fear, a sense of unknown horrors stalking through the alien night.

One Last Word:
To Hell with the Cost!

Samuel Goldwyn, the master of malapropisms ("Whoever pays good money to visit a psychiatrist ought to have his head examined"), is reported, in a typically apocryphal story, to have responded to a complaint that a scenario was "too caustic" by saying:

"Too caustic? To hell with the cost. We'll make the picture anyway."

Today the caustic language comes from doomsayers who proclaim the passing of Hollywood. It is gone, they say; it is no more.

Nonsense!

Hollywood is alive and kicking.

Of course, it has changed. The big studios no longer exist at least in the sense that they once did. No longer are there long rosters of stars under contract.

The studios have lost their power to the biggest of the big stars, who can demand a percentage of the take, and to the directors, whose names may draw an audience more than the actors' do.

But new stars are flickering into sight every year in movies and television is creating a whole new kind of star. Who needs the phony hoopla of the old studio flacks? A Dustin Hoffman can make it and still be what he wants to be—something never permitted in the old days. Imagine a studio boss trying to create a new image for Woody Allen!

Hollywood is still the show business capital of the world. Hollywood and Vine may be a sleazy intersection, but it always was. If the shabby buildings along Hollywood Boulevard weren't painted such a dismal sandy color, we might not be able to contrast them as well with the sun-drenched whiteness of the palatial estates along Sunset Boulevard in Beverly Hills.

Television viewers and movie fans from all over the world still go to Hollywood, and they still hope to see a star. They usually *do* see some actor or actress whose face they recognize, but usually they can't remember the name. But that's all right; they'll fake it when they get back to Chillicothe.

Schwab's Drug Store is still as busy as it was in the days when Walter Winchell was mentioning it every other day. The earnest young men and women, now in frayed jeans and sandals, still congregate in the cinema book stores to talk with solemn passion about film techniques. The lectures go on at the American Film Institute, and the questions are as knowing and probing as ever.

The biggest difference between the old days and contemporary Hollywood is realism, not necessarily on the screen (although there is probably more realism there than there used to be), but in the attitude of the public toward Hollywood. Oscar Levant once said, "Strip away the phony tinsel of Hollywood and you find the real tinsel underneath."

Today the American public is willing to accept that sour truth. Tinsel Town is still just that, but the public knows it, and accepts it as part of the nature of show business. Movie stars are no longer regarded as gods and goddesses; they are people, who behave like people, with all that implies for good and ill.

This more rational attitude, combined with a new candor and common sense about human behavior, especially sexual, has made life much more comfortable for people in Hollywood than it used to be.

Of course, from time to time some politician is bound to come to the decision that he is fit to cast the first stone, to judge the quality of an artist's work by the state of the artist's morals. But that is part of the circus that is American public life.

When that happens next, it would be well for all of us to bear in mind that an investigation of Washington's morals could probably uncover more sin than Hollywood harbors. But Hollywood doesn't investigate Washington.

Maybe that's what's wrong with *both* Washington and Hollywood.